DIEGO'S GUITAR

BOOK THREE OF THE RELUCTANT PILGRIM SERIES

STEPHEN R. MARRIOTT

THE MARSH BOOKS

CONTENTS

JOIN MY NEWSLETTER

Have you joined my author's community yet? Members are always the first to hear about my new books and other cool things I think you'll like.

I send free monthly newsletters about my discoveries along the way (I travel a lot and live in my van part of the year) including travel tips, book recommendations and off the beaten path experiences. Plus, occasional emails with details of new publications, free books and community events.

See the back of the book for details of how to sign up.

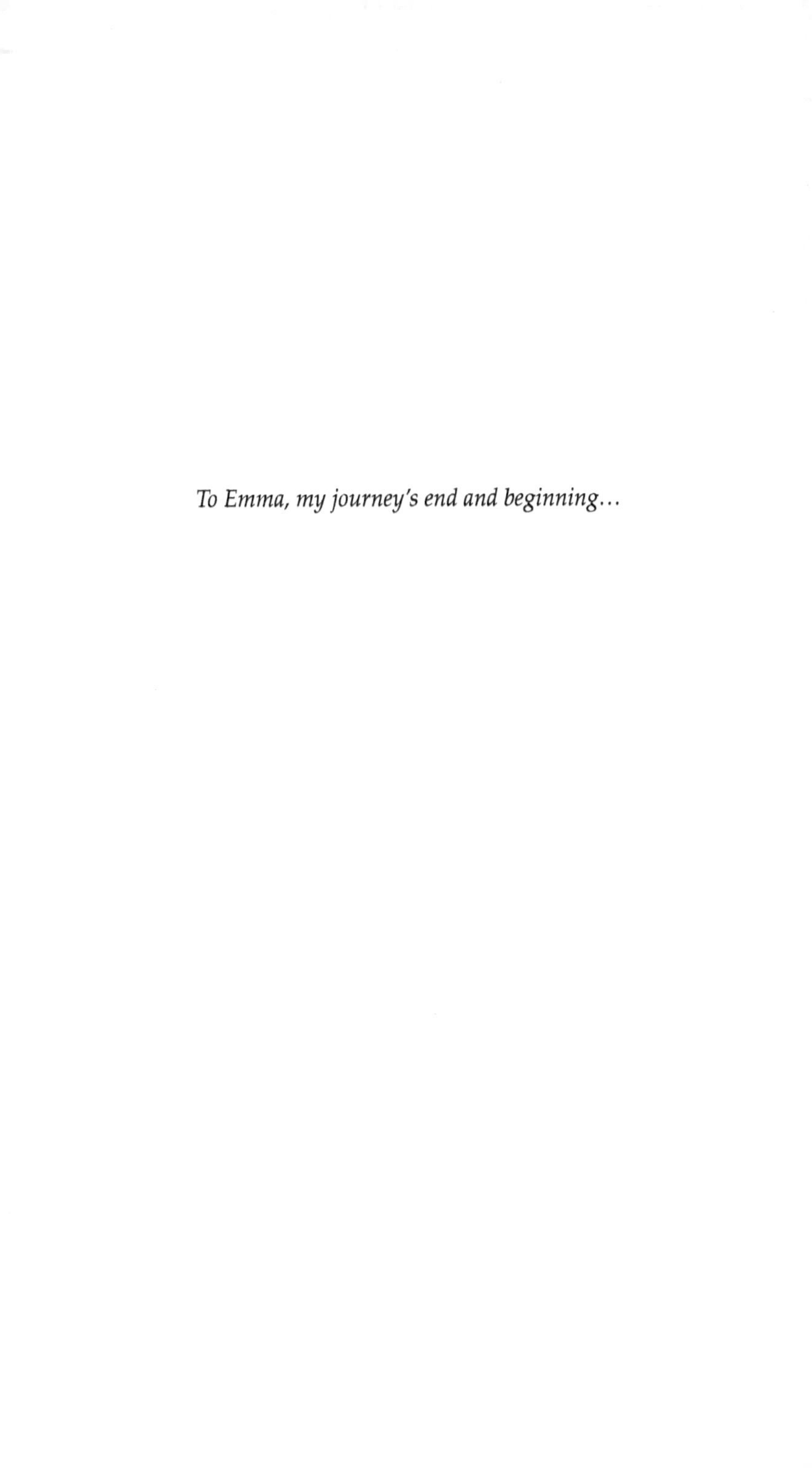

To Emma, my journey's end and beginning…

And I went down the trail with her,
With the twinkling stars to guide me,
For they alone know the path.

– Rosalía de Castro,
from *Flight To Wonderland*
(translated by Eduardo Freire Canosa)

Fisterra
Santiago de Compostela
Vilagarcía de Arousa
Pontevedra
Tui
Valença
SPAIN
PORTUGAL
Ponte de Lima
Viana do Castelo
Vila do Conde
Porto
N
W E
S

D*iego,*

I'm sorry to have to tell you this way, but things are not right between us. And I'm fed up pretending that they are. So, I think we should get a divorce. I waited up half the night for you to return to talk, and when you didn't come back, again, I became sure I was doing the right thing by leaving. I thought over those dreams of travelling around the world and how I once believed they were your dreams too. Because that was how you presented yourself when you returned from your Camino. Those nine years ago. Full of the stories of your walking adventure, you carried an air of belief and possibility.

You made me believe there was another way, and we could see the world together – it was a good story. I bought into it. And I was prepared to wait so you could finish studying flamenco. After you dropped your music lessons, you expected me to be patient again as you pursued your rock career. But I don't think you ever comprehended how lonely this was for me; you were always away on tour or working late in the studio. When you were around there were the parties and your drinking escapades. And to make things worse, you never seemed satisfied! If you couldn't be happy with the fulfilment of your dreams, how about letting me try to fulfil mine?

We had some great times together, and I'll treasure them. But I am not getting any younger and I cannot put my life on hold anymore for you. I will appoint a lawyer to make the arrangements. Please wait for them to get in touch, as we shouldn't be in contact at the moment. I don't want you to try and dissuade me. Plus, I need my space right now, so please respect that. Diego, you will be okay without me. You're talented, smart and still young.

Good luck with the tour,
Mari

PART I

1

INFERNO

The crowded music venue swayed as an ageing Latino rock legend, Carlos Pepi, performed his trademark electric guitar solo. Diego arrived backstage clenching a bottle of Super Bock beer. He wanted to sense the atmosphere, but also needed time to compose himself before taking centre stage. The rock star was doing his job well, lifting the emotions of the crowd, but also leaving room for Diego's performance to raise the roof.

The outline of a tall man trailed down the dimly lit corridor and appeared beside Diego. He unbuttoned the blazer of his sharp suit. "It's a sell-out crowd, Diego." The man was in his early thirties and had chiselled features, with his hair clipped short and tight. His accent was deliberately English Home Counties, although a trained ear would have noticed his northern roots.

I'm a sell-out, thought Diego. "You expect anything less, Marco?"

"No, just rooting for us." Mark studied Diego's profile. "You're not nervous are you?"

Diego's heart was pounding. He took a deep breath. "No. Well, maybe just a little."

Mark slapped Diego on the shoulder. "Good man. We're going to make a mint on this tour." And turning back down the corridor, added, "don't screw this up!"

Diego felt the urge to punch him, but kept his emotions in check and cast a glance at Pepi, who was pacing around the stage. *Bet he never had to put up with any of that shit from his manager*, he thought. Fleetingly, his eyes were drawn off stage to the profile of a slim figure in a low-cut dress talking into the ear of a security man. Amongst the blur of the crowd and in the dark, he couldn't properly identify her, although her shape looked familiar. He took a slug of his beer and then put it down on a redundant speaker. Occasionally, Mari had turned up unexpectedly at his concerts, and although it had sometimes thrown him off-kilter a little, this time he felt relieved to see her. *¡Madre mia! She's changed her mind*, Diego thought hopefully, as he paced towards the steps leading down to the crowd.

He approached the security man, whose large frame was shielding the woman. Diego collected his thoughts, thinking about how he might explain his way out of another one of his screw ups. Blaming Mark was an option, although that excuse was wearing thin. He figured simply saying, "sorry" without complicating things was his best option at that moment. "She's my wife, she can come backstage," said Diego, addressing the security man and not the woman he shaded.

The burly man turned around, stepping to one side and unblocking Diego's view of the slim woman. Immediately he realised she wasn't Mari. "What?" said the man gruffly, not initially recognising Diego.

The woman smiled excitedly at Diego as she snatched her phone from her petite shoulder bag.

"Sorry, thought I recognised her." He tapped the man on his thick shoulder and continued, "You're doing a fine job. *Gracias.*"

The woman gestured at Diego with her phone, and he

acknowledged her with a forced half-smile. In a moment she was beside him, her arm wrapped around his leather jacket and *cerveza* belly, and with her other hand snapped a selfie. Diego nodded at her and the man before retreating up the steps to his side of the stage. The crowd began to applaud as Pepi and his group finished their set. Diego's band members and Mark gathered at the edge of the stage and momentarily the lights dimmed before the PA vibrated around the auditorium announcing Diego "el Relámpago" and his band.

Thousands of screams echoed around the auditorium as they entered the stage before it fell into darkness again. In the momentary stillness, Diego reached for his guitar from its stand. Seconds later a blue halo encircled him, and his tobacco-stained Stratocaster now hung over his shoulder. A swirling studio light briefly shone across the woman he'd mistaken for Mari, and Diego noticed her running a hand through her dark fringe. He returned his attention to the guitar and routinely fingered its strings. His music burning with the old gypsy fire, as he stoked his electric guitar. The halo followed him as he strode towards the edge of the stage.

Diego tipped his Stetson at the audience and raised his arm in the air. The crowd responded with hysterical cries. He strummed his strings, and the heavy metallic notes of a bass guitar joined his electric tones while drums exploded into frenzied thunder rolls. To the rear, sparkling pyrotechnic pillars, the shape of poplar trees, fizzed high. A pianist slid his hand from one end of his synthesiser to the other; a chorus of trombones entered the fray and the backing vocalists cupped their hands together in a gesture to traditional flamenco handclapping, *palmas*.

The stage turned a golden yellow and a stringy youth gripping a microphone and wearing a beanie hat slithered across it towards Diego. He raised his eyebrows knowingly at the singer. They leaned into each other. Diego's fingers brushed the strings, rumba style, and the man began to rap. The backing vocalists emphasising, "*Mamacita*".

> *Hey girl pick up the receiva,*
> *I've been trying to reach ya?*
> *Mamacita*
> *Don't want to cheat ya,*
> *Jus' I wanna meet ya*
> *Can't you see, my Mamacita,*
> *I've got a feva for your flava*
> *No time to save it for another,*
> *yo girl I'm here!*
> *I'm your lover,*
> *come little mother, Mamacita,*
> *let me meet ya*
> *Let me treat ya*
> *to a midnight carnival*
> *Come on Mama,*
> *I'm your nirvana on a Honda*
> *No way this hasta la vista…*

Diego's guitar hung loosely around his shoulder as he picked casually on the strings, his eyes blurring across the crowd as he played back in his head the events of two nights before.

He'd been looking out at the streets of his one-time stomping ground, Barrio de La Latina. Smoking a cigarette and feeling ready to leave the after-party to have that talk he'd promised Mari. Musing how he'd once hustled those Madrid streets; recalling his dawn strolls after pulling an all-nighter in Copas Anton, the basement flamenco bar. He remembered the smell of baking bread and the morning song of birds. A time when no one wanted a piece of him, and his music was as pure as the *Aubades* of those waking birds. But Mark had caught him outside the restaurant and distracted his reflections and thoughts of departure. Insisting he needed to walk the party some more and have his photo taken with his carefully selected guests.

"Come on, mate, you gotta do your bit of PR for the tour. Just one more drink, Lightning Boy. The label's paying. Besides, you got a day off before we hit Porto and set the world on fire," was all it had taken to get Diego back into the restaurant. That act was the final straw for Mari. Later, in the early hours, he'd staggered into their apartment and discovered her letter beside the fruit bowl. Her words were confirmed by her absence, and the swinging clothes hangers in their wardrobe. *Estúpido, how stupid of me. ¡Gilipollas!* Diego thought, as he continued to reproach himself. *All I had to do was say no.*

His eyes were drawn to a glowing exit sign at the back of the auditorium. It cast a pale green light over a closed door. The door opened and a thickset figure came out of the darkness and stood illuminated in the ghostly light. It made him think of a street vendor from his childhood days on fiesta night, stood under one of the old gas lamps that had remained in his village. The figure stopped short of the first step down and shook his head slowly. In the pallid glow, Diego thought he was looking at his deceased papá. The old man began to shake his head and, stretching his gaze further towards him, Diego could see his face was full of the wrinkles of flamenco. Was it his former guitar maestro, shaking his head? Diego squinted down at his fingers, now quivering over the strings of his guitar. His whole body was trembling. He looked back up, but all he now saw was the exit door swinging back on its hinges. But he understood the message from the elderly man, whoever he was. The slow motion of his disapproving head and the heavy door closing had said it all. *No más*, no more. You're better than this.

The tapping heels of rosewood echoing across the stage jolted Diego's attention. Automatically, he and the rapper stepped to one side, allowing a flamenco dancer to stand in the centre of the stage. She was wearing a lipstick-red leather jacket and hard-hitting flamenco shoes. The dancer contorted her arms upwards with her palms bent out, arching like the limbs of a windswept tree. Standing high on her heels, a quick twist saw her body spin effortlessly around, and the youthful singer patted his microphone, babbling into it, "*Mamacita, Olé, Olé...*"

What the hell am I doing? Diego asked himself, as he angled the neck of his guitar preparing to pluck long, redemptive synthesised tones, familiar to a thousand rock guitar solos. *This isn't my music.*

He felt compelled to run, to breathe. "*¡Qué cabrón!*" he cursed as he glared at his audience. Suddenly Diego grabbed his guitar by its neck and a high-pitched buzz vibrated around the auditorium. He turned to face the speakers, pausing before taking a step toward them. Next, he raised the guitar high above his head, approached the speakers and swung it into them. The speakers crackled and Diego felt an electric shock burning him. He relaxed his grip on the guitar and it pounded the floor. The speakers began smoking.

Diego glanced across to the wings, flipped Mark the finger and trotted off the stage. The crowd booed. He picked up his pace along the corridor, heading towards the stage door. He was already flagging down a passing taxi by the time Mark had reached the exit. The taxi stopped, Diego dived in. He slid down into the back seats and didn't look back at Mark sheltering from the rain in the doorway. After a minute or two had passed, Diego sat up. He fumbled around in the pockets of his jacket. Finding the crumpled letter, he began to reread it.

2

THE RAILWAY STATION

It was tempting to read the letter a further time. As if by rereading it, its tone might have softened. Perhaps he would find some clues previously missed, suggesting Mari had been wavering in her decision. But he folded it and returned it to his jacket. Acknowledging the events of two nights ago couldn't be undone, and for the moment, at least, Mari was gone. Then he noticed his fretting hand had reddened from the electric shock; he checked it closer. His fingertips down to his palm had turned almost lobster pink. He scrunched his hand and became aware of the lashing of heavy rainfall on tarmac outside.

Diego peered out of the window, still with no idea of where to tell the driver to take him. His eyes traced the lines of rain smearing down the long windows of cafés and bars. People crowded inside them; fleetingly Diego sensed the authenticity in their trivial curiosities and conversation. Chatter about the weather, work, sport and such like. He ran the thumb of his right hand across a corner of the misting window and smoothed the condensation across the back of his marked fingers. Stretching them at the joints, they still felt as flexible as spider legs, albeit a little numb.

Diego asked the taxi driver to take him to a late-night pharmacy and wait for him. At the pharmacy Diego purchased arnica gel, and leaving he paused in the doorway, observing São Bento railway station across the street. It was an unshakable three-storey building, although blue blemishes of light in its vaulted windows softened its granite facade. Rain slanted in the lights of waiting taxis and to the side of the building, he noticed a man gathering tables and chairs together and running a chain around them. Diego detected a place of sanctuary to gather his thoughts. He turned the collar of his leather jacket up, dashed over to the taxi and paid the driver. He breathed in the damp night air before hurrying across the street and ducking into the station bar.

The place was dim and musty and appealed to his senses. Behind the bar counter was the man he'd spotted from his viewpoint at the pharmacy doorway. He was gangly, stood a little stooped, and dried his young face and cropped hair with a hand towel. The only other occupant was a fair-haired girl who briefly looked up from her guidebook and half-smiled at Diego. He nodded subtly in reply before his eyes crept to the rows of spirits behind the barman, alighting on a bottle of Scotch whisky. The barman served him a double and nodded courteously when Diego shook his head at the idea of cutting it with water or ice.

Moving over to the corner of the bar, Diego pulled out a chair at a table beside a cigarette machine and, shaking the rain from his hat, sat down. Sipping on the whisky, he tasted its earthiness and it brought him some comfort. The arnica, however, was the best medicine. Immediately after applying the gel to his hand, it began soothing his fingers. He started to calm, although he couldn't work out his next move, reckoning all options would result in discomfort one way or another. The prospect of returning to Madrid and searching for Mari would go against her wishes, most likely making things worse. And the idea of facing Mark back at the hotel made him half sick to his stomach. He couldn't deal with all his money-loving panic. Nevertheless, he wasn't absolutely sure if he was ready to get off the gravy train, just yet. He knocked back his whisky and ordered another double.

Delivering Diego's whisky, the young barman looked down at his bedraggled appearance and damp hat, and casually remarked, "It's an awful night."

Diego looked up. "*Sí*, it's ugly!"

The barman glanced towards the door leading through to the station and the platforms and said, "Kind of night that makes you want to jump on the next train and get the hell out of here."

Diego couldn't help but smile. "You don't like working here, then?"

"There's nothing wrong with it, but I guess working at a train station gives you ideas."

Diego leaned back on his chair, and catching the barman's gaze he saw a little of his younger self in the man's preoccupied eyes. He corrected his chair and something in that intimate moment led him to invite the barman to leave the bottle of whisky on his table and join him in a drink. Initially, he hesitated and glanced around at the near-empty bar. But seeing the girl was preoccupied with her book he grabbed a whisky glass and drew out a chair.

"Is this your only job?" asked Diego.

"Yes, it's part-time. I'm a student."

"What are you studying?"

"Architecture."

"Nice city to study architecture, I bet? I haven't seen much, but I did notice there are some beautiful buildings in the centre."

"Porto used to have many more, but you probably noticed the cranes too. A lot of work for an architect if you don't mind ripping the heart out of the old buildings!"

"Hmm, I get the feeling you're not sure about your future line of work?"

The barman took a sip of his whisky as he thought over Diego's statement. He put his glass down. "Well, I'm doing it for the family. My old man has an architectural practice and he sees me running it one day. I'm an only child, you see, and when he retires he expects me to take it over."

Diego topped up their glasses and asked, "Does he even know you've got this job?"

The barman frowned. "No, he thinks I'm studying at the university library most nights." He glanced at Diego's Stetson again, then regarded him curiously. "And what do you do?"

"That's a good question. If you'd asked me that around an hour ago I could have given you a definitive answer."

The barman eyed Diego further. "I know you! Aren't you Diego Relámpago?"

Diego took a long sip of his whisky and eventually replied, "You've got me there."

"Thought you were performing at the Colisea tonight?"

"It was cancelled, a problem with the electrics."

"Oh?"

"So you've heard of me?"

"Of course, I bought your first CD."

"Just the first one?"

"Um, well," mumbled the barman squirming in his chair. "You see I'm more into the acoustic guitar than rock."

Diego put his glass down, sighed and lowered his voice. "That's okay, I think I am too." Speaking up he asked, "You play?"

The barman reached for his glass and nodded. "Yes, but my father thinks it's a waste of good study time." He took a sip of whisky, and then continued, "When it's quiet I sometimes practice here. I have a guitar behind the bar."

"That's great."

"Not sure my father would agree with you."

"Well that's okay, we don't all share the same dreams."

The barman frowned again. "Ha, dreams, what's the point!"

"Are you speaking for your father?"

"Um…"

"…Remember it was you who suggested the idea of jumping on the next train out of here."

"But the business is my father's legacy."

"But your dreams aren't bound by your papá. Tell me this, is his business successful?"

"It is."

"Well, perhaps the business has already reached its potential?"

A youthful group spilled into the bar and distracted the barman's attention. He looked at his watch and avoided answering Diego's question. "They'll be wanting a final drink before they catch their train." He stood up and returned to the counter to serve the customers.

Diego noticed one of them was wearing a T-shirt with his el Relámpago rock star image splashed across its front, his tour dates on its back. He realised they must have been at his abandoned concert. He lowered his head, but almost immediately someone shouting from across the bar noticed him.

"Hey man, you suck!" Diego looked back up. "It *is* you," yelled the man in the T-shirt. He nudged his friend and pointed at Diego. "It's him, Diego Relámpago!" He yelled at Diego again. "You ought to buy us all drinks for the money we lost on tickets to your show."

Diego dug a hand into a pocket of his jeans, thinking that indeed money might resolve things. But with his leather wallet in hand, he felt a new set of eyes on him. He looked up to see the fair-haired girl had put her book down and was staring at him. Her eyes were narrow, though they glinted with curiosity. Straightaway, a different notion came to him and he put his wallet away. He poured some more whisky into his glass and threw it back. He coughed, shook his hat out and returned it to his head. Then he stood up, stepped across to the bar and said to the barman, "Hey, do you have your guitar with you tonight?"

"Yes?" he replied, midway through pouring a beer.

"Can I borrow it?"

The barman put the glass down. "Sure," he replied, reaching down behind the bar. He found his Spanish guitar and passed it over the counter to Diego.

It was cedar red and felt lightweight in his hands. Diego nodded at the barman and said, "Remember my older style?"

"*Si, Señor.*"

Diego turned to confront his small gathering of fans and said, "I'll do something better than compensating you all with drinks. I'll give you a private show right here in this bar. None of that YouTube rapsturbating shit the label is forcing me to play." They stared back at him bemused.

The fair-haired girl stood up and pulled out a chair at her table, turning it to face the bar. With a Welsh twang, she said, "Are you going to wait there, or are you going to play your music?"

"Thanks," said Diego. He joined the Welsh girl, sat down and faced the fans. He rested the guitar on his lap, tilted his head over the soundboard and plucked a low E. It sounded mournful, yet resilient, and only required a small adjustment of its tuning peg. The other strings required minimal tuning too. He took a breath, and in that momentary stillness, the early teachings of his maestro came to mind, whereby, the professor would have Diego mimicking the classic flamenco guitarists before allowing his own emotions to seep in. He felt the urge to play his favourite Paco de Lucia song, *Between Two Waters*. When he began, his notes played crisp and fine and he felt no pain in his burnt fingers. Diego upped the pace of his *picado*, his middle fingers galloping along the strings.

He glanced up at his fans, looking for approval. The Tshirted man had folded his arms and was leaning into the bar, while his friend, a twenty-something male with ruffled hair, nonchalantly sipped from his beer bottle. They were with a couple of girls, who appeared indifferent to the music. Just two older-looking guys watched with mild fascination.

Screw this, thought Diego. *If they're going to show me the door I might as well play how I want.* He paused and removed a silver cigarette case from an inside pocket of his jacket and withdrew a long Marlboro, tapping its butt against the metal. He searched his pockets for a lighter, but the Welsh girl stretched her hand across the table and lit his cigarette with her own lighter. Diego glanced up at the barman, gesturing with his cigarette. The youth nodded back approvingly and Diego took a puff, then angled it in his mouth.

He closed his eyes and almost immediately felt at peace; his fingers calmed and he began to play a rumba. His head nodded up and down, reflecting on those dawn song Madrid streets. He slowly released more energy into the strings, his melody telling the story of those waking birds, flamenco feathers fluffing with the aroma of baking bread rising above the rooftops.

Cries of "¡Olé, Olé!" and the cupping of hands broke Diego's trance and he opened his eyes to see ecstatic faces now seized by his music. His fingers continued to run freely across the strings and he played on. After improvising a couple more songs and observing the gathering bashing their beer bottles on the bar and crashing their feet on the floor, Diego decided that calming things down and buying everyone a round of drinks wouldn't do any harm after all. He brought his music to an end and everyone applauded.

The girl leaned across the table and whispered in Diego's ear, "That was lush!"

"What?"

"Your music was excellent."

"Oh, thanks," replied Diego, resting the guitar on his lap. "Can I get you a drink?"

"No, let me buy you one."

"Well, I'm going to buy a round for everyone anyhow."

"I insist. Really, you deserve it. What's your tipple?"

"You're a stubborn one!"

She stared firmly back at him and, defeated, Diego said, "A beer would go down well."

"Lush," she replied, standing up from the table.

Diego winked. "That I am."

Immediately, the man in the T-shirt and several of the fans gathered around Diego and took numerous selfies with him on their phones. Afterwards, he broke away from them and went up to the bar where the Welsh girl was now standing. Diego returned the guitar to the barman. Receiving it, he said, "You didn't learn to play that in university, did you?"

"Ha, no, but I've had numerous lessons."

"Ah, I see. *Obrigado!*"

"For what?"

"Just thanks."

Diego smiled and then ordered the round of drinks. His fans soon joined him at the bar, and he shrugged his shoulders at the Welsh girl as they congregated between them. Several beers later and with the fans departing to catch their last train, Diego leaned into the bar counter and said to the girl, "I never did get your name?"

"It's Vanessa, but everyone calls me Nessie."

"Like the monster," said Diego, with a wink.

"Just like the monster. But far more dangerous," replied Nessie, matching Diego's wink.

"So, Nessie, what brings you here to Porto on your own? And where are my manners? I'm Diego."

"I know who you are, your groupies told me all about you and your concert. Sounds like you've ruffled a few feathers tonight. So I guess I could ask you a similar question. What made you come to this bar and walk out on your gig?"

Diego angled his beer bottle to his lips and drank as he thought. "Rather not talk about it?"

"Fair play, what's life without mystery?"

"Exactly," said Diego clinking his beer bottle against hers.

Nessie took a sip of her beer and Diego stole a glance at her. Her hair was a wispy white-blonde rather than fair, like clouds of candyfloss. Her blue eyes shone brightly against her pale face. She was wearing a light fleece over a white blouse. As she relaxed and rested against the bar counter, she tilted the heels of her walking shoes against the brass-coloured footrest and he realised she was much shorter than him.

"Are you a walker?" he asked.

"What makes you say that?" Diego glanced down at the footrest and she responded, "Ah, my shoes. Actually, I'm walking the Camino Portugués; have you heard of it?"

Diego placed his bottle on the counter. "There's a Camino path from here to Santiago de Compostela?"

"There is."

"Ah, you were reading a Camino guidebook earlier?"

"You're good!" she said glancing back at their table and her guidebook. "Lovely, it's still there."

"Hmm, I once walked it, actually a couple of its trails. You start tomorrow?"

"Yes."

"You'll have an adventure for sure."

"Hoping to." She tilted her bottle to her lips and drained it.

Diego's dark eyes held hers firmly. "You don't mess around!"

"Well, I just realised I better get some sleep."

"You'd better."

"What are you going to do?" asked Nessie.

Diego glugged the remains of his beer. "Not sure. Guess I'll find another hotel, best I avoid mine tonight."

"You can stay at my hotel if you like? It's only around the corner."

Diego raised his eyebrows.

"I didn't mean it like that; they gave me a twin room."

"That's good because I'm married. But a spare bed you say? Tempting, very tempting."

"Well, it's available, with clean sheets and all."

"You're sure?"

"Come on. I'm not going to make a mess of your wedding vows."

Diego reached out a hand. "Fair enough. *Gracias*. You're a lifesaver." They shook hands and Nessie collected her book from the table.

"That was an extraordinary night," the barman said grinning at Diego.

Diego adjusted his hat, and replied, "Very unexpected."

He glanced through the window, past the entrance hall decorated by panels of *azulejos*, painted tiles depicting views of Portuguese history, and beyond the glaucous platforms towards the darkness. Nessie tapped his arm, breaking his vision. He nodded back at the barman and his gesture might have been interpreted as Diego saying to him: "You'll find your way," even though he had no idea where his own life was now heading. Nessie grabbed hold of Diego's arm, steadying him as they left.

The young barman collected some empty glasses from a table and passing by the window, he paused, casting a thoughtful look through it as his eyes wandered across the empty platforms.

3

CAMINO BREEZE

Dawn sunlight streaking across Diego's face awoke him. The slats of the shutters had not been fully closed, creating a pattern of light and dark stripes across his lengthy frame. He was lying above the covers of the single bed, and he lifted an arm to look at his watch. Squinting at the face of his Rolex, he learned it was 07:09. He looked across at Nessie sleeping peacefully in the adjacent bed. Besides a vague memory of arriving at the hotel, Diego didn't remember much beyond that. He was still wearing his burgundy silk shirt and designer jeans, although his jacket and boots had been removed. He sat up and noticed his mobile phone on the bedside table and was grateful he'd turned it to sleep mode ahead of the concert.

Instinctively he reached for it. There were several voice and text messages from Mark, but he skipped to the message from Gracia, his Personal Assistant. Concern about his whereabouts was the gist of Gracia's text, and although he felt duty-bound to reassure her, he couldn't face being in touch with her just yet; no doubt Mark would be pressing Gracia hard for any information she might have. However, the phone was absent of any messages from the one person Diego wanted to hear from.

He turned off the phone and glanced back at Nessie. She was still sleeping. He slid off the bed and crept into the bathroom. He stuck his head under the tap of the little washbasin and gulped down some water then inspected his fretting fingers, admiring the fast work of the arnica in healing his hand. The blemishes had almost gone. The only pain he felt now was in his head. He peed at length, threw off his clothes and took a shower. His thoughts remained as dull as the low-pressure water from the shower. Drinking a coffee and smoking a cigarette was all he could think of doing next.

When he got out of the shower Diego examined himself in the mirror above the washbasin. He scowled at his tired eyes and frown lines. Then he stood back, turned to one side and angled his torso towards the mirror. There was no hiding his beer belly. He removed his hand from his stomach and ran it through his dark hair. Though it had thinned a little above his temples, overall his wet mop remained thick and reassuring. Feeling a little happier, he took a towel to his hair and dried it, before drying the rest of himself off. While dressing he searched his jeans pockets for a hairband, but he didn't have one.

Returning to the bedroom, Diego found Nessie already up and dressed. "Ah, *buenos días*," he said, a little sheepishly.

"That's good morning in Spanish, right?"

"Sorry, guess I'm still sleepy. But yes, it is."

"Don't apologise. I want to pick up some Spanish. It'll help when I hit the Spanish side of the Camino at Tui."

"*No hay problema.*"

"Ha, I can work that one out."

Diego glimpsed at her shoulder-length hair and said, "You don't have a spare hairband by chance?"

"I might do. Let me check my wash bag in the bathroom."

A few minutes later, Nessie returned from the bathroom

and handed Diego a hairband, and he subsequently pulled his mane back into a ponytail. Nessie was eager to start her walk, but they agreed to take breakfast together at a café before they went their separate ways. The receptionist pointed them in the direction of the city's cathedral, the starting point for pilgrims walking the Camino Portugués from Porto. And also the place to obtain a *credencial* – the pilgrim passport.

Diego and Nessie strolled along the city's backstreets as swifts swooped between the tiled rooftops above. Diego walked with a tipped head, whereas Nessie's bright cotton sun hat bobbed casually, riding high on hers. She wore distinctive green leggings and was carrying a lavender pack, giving her the air of a backpacker going to the beach. The streets were still damp from the rain the night before and in a tiled section of paving, Diego spotted a yellow Camino arrow and shell. The marker was distinctive yet camouflaged amongst the cobbles, to those not looking for direction. A winching sound attracted their attention and they glimpsed a tall man in the autumn years of his life winding out the canopy outside his storefront. Above, the words: Farmácia Independente were painted in a bold blue script across pale tiles, edged by rectangular ones with a floral design. Diego went inside and bought himself a bottle of water. They passed more shops and houses, their facades also decorated by the ubiquitous *azulejos* tiles.

They soon arrived at a pedestrianised street of stores below terraces of lofty apartment blocks. Wedged between a florist and a gift shop was a café with tables outside. They grabbed a spare one, ordered coffees and croissants and lit up. Nessie noticed that Diego's smoking hand was a little shaky, but she didn't say anything. He was gazing up at the swifts and appeared distant. The arrival of their coffees and pastries did little to ease Diego's preoccupied mind. It was the jarring sounds of a shutter opening across the entrance to an outdoor sports store that finally shook him out of his trance. Nessie looked over her shoulder and smiled.

"That's handy, I'll pop in there after, and see's if they have any Kendal Mint Cake."

"Kendal Mint Cake?"

"It's popular with walkers in the UK, but I'd eat it whenever, to be honest. I love mint."

"Sounds nice." Diego stirred his coffee a couple of times, and then said, "We didn't do anything last night, did we?"

Nessie feigned a surprised expression. "How could you forget? I thought we had a cracking night. You don't remember anything about it!?"

"Err?"

Nessie began laughing. "I'm just teasing you, Diego. You passed out almost as soon as you sat on the bed."

"Oh? Sorry."

"That's okay. Your wife must love you!"

"You removed my boots?"

"I did. You were snoring like a rock star!"

"Hmm, how fitting."

Nessie's smirk curled into a sympathetic smile. "Guess it was a long day for you. But your performance in the bar was very cool. And it's not even your normal style?"

"What do you mean?"

"The acoustic guitar, the solo performance. I'm afraid I don't know your music, but your fans said you're a big stage performer and famous in Spain and Portugal."

"Well yes, but that Spanish guitar took me back to my roots. I don't know what Marco or the record company would say…"

"Marco?"

"He's my manager, Mark. Ha, I'd love to see his face at the moment. He must be seething back at the hotel."

"You don't get on with him?"

"Well, let's just say he's got one hell of an attitude." Diego took a drag of his cigarette, and then added, "Well it might not even matter now. Storming off the stage like that might prove to be one of the most stupid things I've ever done. But man, it felt good. Though I'm not sure what my wife is going to think about my stunt either."

"I get it. Packing my rucksack and buying an airline ticket gave me enormous satisfaction." Nessie took a thoughtful drag on her cigarette, then stretched out her arm, cigarette in hand. "You see my boyfriend didn't want me to go on this walk alone."

"So you're with someone?" Nessie nodded. "Good for you, though – having the courage to walk it alone."

"Maybe, but my boyfriend thinks he should be here with me, protecting me from any hazards that may come my way. What he doesn't realise is that I need to know I'm capable. You know – reaching Santiago on my own, dealing with whatever comes round the corner."

Diego added some sugar to his coffee. "You've thought this over somewhat?" Nessie nodded and took a sip of coffee. Diego continued, "Without Marco and the record company, I'd be nothing."

"You're going to continue the tour then?"

"Not sure, can't really explain what's going on inside my head right now." Diego looked up from his coffee and gazed down the street.

Sensing his despondence, Nessie decided changing the subject might help. "Any tips for walking the Camino?"

He took a bite of his croissant and chewed over the question. "Take your time walking it. You want to remember the experience."

"Sounds great, but I've got a bit of a deadline now, as my boyfriend is meeting me in Tui."

"Thought you were planning on walking it without him?"

"Well, I'll have around a week on my own, so that's something I guess?"

"What happened?"

"He texted me yesterday afternoon, shortly after I arrived. He was meant to be having two weeks on holiday with his mate, but he's changed his plans and cut it short. So he said he'll meet me there, in Tui."

Leaning back, Diego blew a smoke ring into the air. "Hmm, does he like walking?"

"Not really," replied Nessie glumly, reaching for her croissant. "The outdoors isn't his thing." She raised her eyebrows. "But what about you? When did you walk the Camino?"

Diego got the message and grinned. "*Sí*, let's talk about me. It's a much more interesting subject. Now let me think…" Diego generally marked the passage of time by the strides in life he'd made with Mari. Checking the date on his watch, he realised it would be their fifth wedding anniversary in ten days, marking nine years of them being together. "It must have been over nine years ago now, given it's the third week of August."

Nessie tore off a piece of her pastry. "You need some time to figure things out, right?"

"Probably."

"Well, why don't you walk another Camino?"

Diego squinted curiously at Nessie. "Are you asking me to walk with you?"

Nessie put her croissant on her plate and grinned. "Well, I reckon I can trust you, given your inability to stay awake as soon as you enter a girl's bedroom." She glanced over her shoulder at the outdoor store. "You could buy some decent walking boots there. Don't reckon your sissy shitkickers would last long on the trail."

"Whoa, easy does it, Nessie! These boots cost me six hundred dollars – handmade in Mexico. What's good enough for Clint Eastwood is good enough for me."

Nessie responded with a teasing grin, and in that moment, a summer breeze brushed his cheeks and Diego sensed the moist, humid atmosphere of the early mornings of the Galician stretch of his first Camino walk. Suddenly, he was overcome with the need to walk and fill his pilgrim lungs, thinking that chatting with Nessie along the route might help distract him from his current quandary. *But I mustn't*, he thought. *I need my sleeping pills and what if I can't get a drink?*

"*Loco*," he exclaimed out loud.

"I know that word! No crazier than a Welsh girl from the valleys jumping on a plane, and telling her boyfriend she's going to walk through a foreign country?"

"Maybe not."

"When's your next gig?"

"In three days, in Lisbon."

"Maybe that's all the time you need to sort your head out?"

"Perhaps. It'd be one way to lay low for a couple of days. Let me think about it while I let someone know I'm okay, and ask them to take care of some things for me. Whatever happens I can't face returning to my hotel and the shit storm I must have created there."

Diego turned his phone back on to message Gracia; he first looked to see if there were any messages from Mari, but she hadn't contacted him. He delayed typing his text and looked at Nessie to catch her fleeting smile. And for the first time, he fully appreciated her beauty. Nessie was as healthy and bright as a flowering spring hedgerow. Diego took a deep breath and texted Gracia. He explained he was okay, asked her to invent one of her famous excuses and put Mark off, and said that she would hear from him before the Lisbon concert. In the meantime, she should pack up his things in his hotel room and enjoy Porto for a couple of days; but above everything else, not worry.

Writing the text and buying himself time had the effect of calming Diego's nerves and he found himself saying, "Reckon

I'm up for a change of scenery. *Gracias*, I will join you for a couple of days walking."

"Lush!"

Diego settled their bill before they crossed over to the outdoor shop. He purchased a backpack, sleeping bag, pair of socks and at the last minute added a hip flask to his gear. To Nessie's delight, she found some Kendal Mint Cake bars. Outside they arranged to split up briefly, so Diego could go back to the pharmacy and pick up some necessities. That would also give Nessie time to get her pilgrim *credencial* at the cathedral. According to the directions, the cathedral wasn't too far away; just further along the street and up a hill.

At the pharmacy Diego bought a toothbrush, toothpaste, deodorant and the strongest sleeping pills they would sell him. Then, passing a convenience store, he nipped in and bought himself a bottle of scotch before ducking into an alley and filling his hip flask with the whisky. Then he was on his way, guiding himself up the steep slopes of the city towards the cathedral.

4

LEAVING PORTO

The lengthy shadow ascended the final steps into the plaza. Diego directed himself to a stone wall and dropped his khaki backpack as he steadied himself against the wall. He didn't care to look behind and take in the view. Had he done so, he would have gazed across red-tiled rooftops, descending into the haze of the lower city, glimpsing the leafy green waters of Porto's Rio Douro lapping westward. North was the Spanish border, and then Santiago.

The tassels on the arms of Diego's leather jacket flapped in the breeze. He tilted the wide brim of his Stetson over his squinting eyes as he gazed at the flagstone plaza and a line of people trailing outside the tourist entrance of the cathedral. He didn't see Nessie amongst them. He wavered, looking for a clear reason to change his mind. Numerous ones came to him but putting some distance between himself and Mark and the record company continued to outweigh them all. Furthermore, Nessie was waiting for him somewhere in the cathedral, and he had to admit he was drawn to her sassy spirit. He slid a hand inside his jacket, pulled out his hip flask and took a long draw on it. Then he shouldered his backpack.

His eyes were drawn up the cathedral's dull stonework exterior and towards its rose window, bordered by two square towers. For some reason, the large window over-looking the city brought to mind the bulbous, disapproving eyes of his flamenco hero Paco de Lucia when Diego had frequented Copas Anton, the flamenco bar. During those late-night drinking sessions throughout his early days in Madrid. Before he was a rock star, he'd continually felt those eyes gazing out of the photo frame and judging his every move.

Diego arrived at the tourist entrance to the cathedral, still there was no sign of Nessie. Feeling the day warming up, he followed the tourists into the cathedral.

Inside he glanced up at the high vaulted ceiling, then down at the red carpet leading to a golden altarpiece before catching sight of Nessie's bright backpack. She was gripping her guidebook and looking up at an icon. It was fan-shaped with sunrays bursting behind it. Flanking it were saints mounted on spiralling pillars the colour of cinnamon.

Diego arrived beside Nessie and she jumped as Diego caught her unawares.

"Ah, Diego!"

"Oh, sorry I didn't mean to startle you."

Nessie caught her breath. "That's okay. *Buenos días.*"

"*Buen día, señorita,*" said Diego, tipping his hat and smiling.

"Hats off in church, cowboy," said Nessie, with a mock headmistress frown. "Didn't your mama teach you anything?"

Pain flashed across Diego's face and his smile froze into a grimace. But in less than a second he recovered his composure, then removed his hat and crossed himself with it before rolling his eyes heavenwards. But Nessie had caught the glimmer of pain.

"Diego, I'm so sorry," she said. "I think I said something hurtful."

Diego smiled his biggest stage smile and quickly switched the chord of conversation. "Hey, did you get your *credencial*?"

"Er… yes I did. You don't want to get one?"

"Rock stars don't stay in hostels – so I won't need one, right? Well, we should get going."

Nessie shrugged her shoulders. "Okay then," and turned towards the rose window and the exit. Strolling along the carpet she said, "There are two paths we can take, according to my guidebook."

They descended the steps into the plaza and squinted in the rising sun. Diego replaced his hat. "Hmm, two paths?"

Nessie opened her guidebook, and Diego found himself eyeing her up as she brushed away some errant strands of hair from her eyes. He was attracted to the innocence of her soft face, which contrasted with her determination. Diego guessed she was in her mid-twenties. "Actually, there are four according to the book. Though there are two main routes – Camino Central, the major one, which is more rural, or Camino Costa, which follows the shoreline."

"You've done your homework," said Diego, as he diverted his eyes and glanced down at the map in her book.

"Of course Diego…I've been planning this for ages."

"So what's your preference?"

"I like the idea of the coastal route but my book says it's less waymarked than the Central. So I guess we'd better walk the Central."

"Hmm, sounds like you think the coastal path will be more fun, though?"

"Well, walking beside the sea would be."

"Let's try that one then."

"Okay, why not," agreed Nessie, the edge of her cheeks folding into a smile. She put her book away into a side pouch of her pack.

Diego cocked his head towards the wall he'd earlier been leaning against. "There was a Camino arrow painted… beside the steps over there, where I climbed to reach this plaza. You must have seen it, too? Pointing down and towards the embankment and the river; that has to be the way for the coastal path."

"Make's sense," said Nessie.

"Okay *señorita*, let's go."

As they cut across the square, Nessie considered how it would have looked in medieval times. Her guidebook described it as a place bustling with trade, filled with market stalls, merchants hawking wares. When they reached the steps, she noticed an arrow stencilled on a wall pointing ahead and nodded towards it. Diego raised a hand to the crown of his hat and nodded.

More arrows led them down meandering cobbled lanes, and the path opened up into plazas containing terraced cafés, restaurants and churches. They didn't say much as they walked. Diego's mind was wandering. Was he about to make a huge mistake? His wife had left him and now he was putting his career in jeopardy too. And why hadn't Mari been in touch – surely she must have heard about his stage antics? Nessie was too busy taking in the activity of the old town. It was swarming with tourists and construction activity, and she counted at least a dozen cranes poking above the tall tenements leaning into the hillside. They lost the Camino markers but figured they needed to keep going downhill.

Heading back into the labyrinth, they passed underneath a niche in the wall, unaware it contained a small statue of the "Lord of Good Fortune". The blue shrine was unassuming but legend had it that anyone passing by it would receive good fortune on their journey. Before long, they arrived at the banks of the river. Whilst it was a little cooler beside the water, the wide-open paving radiated the sun's heat, and droplets of sweat trickled down Diego's neck.

They glanced around without success for a Camino arrow but noticed ahead in the distance pilgrims heading west along the riverbank. Nessie set off after them enthusiastically, though Diego hesitated as he caught his breath. He called after her, asking her to wait for him at a café or bar en route. He took a long, deep breath and drank in the scenery. "*¡Madre mía!*" he whispered, feeling how unfit he was. Couples strolled along the banks, chatter rose from tourists taking late breakfasts at restaurant terraces, and the boats went about their business along the shimmering river.

A barefooted boy wearing Speedos and a Captain America T-shirt appeared beside Diego, drawing him out of his daze. He was Diego's chest height and had the look of a Roma. "*Senhor*, a donation… *por favor*?" he asked, pushing forward an upturned baseball cap.

"*¿Para qué?*, what for?" replied Diego.

The boy pointed back along the river up to a steel bridge arching across the river to other boys, who had climbed over the railings and were whipping up an interested crowd below them. One of the boys raised his arms above his head and prepared to dive off. Next, he turned around so his back faced the water. Then he defiantly pushed against the railings and did a backflip. He slid silently into the river like a cormorant diving for a fish. Seconds later, he popped up beside the riverbank. The crowd roared with delight, clapping enthusiastically.

"*Chico*, you do that too?" asked Diego.

The boy nodded. "Most days in the summer."

"You're not scared?"

The boy casually shook his head.

"You live around here?"

"Close," he replied, casting an arm beyond linen-dressed tables to a scruffy ally. Diego caught sight of a woman on the top floor of a tenement hanging a bed sheet across her balcony railings.

"Convenient location."

The boy gave a nonchalant shrug. "Guess so… if you have money," and he stretched out his cap again.

Diego found his wallet and placed twenty Euros into the cap. The boy grabbed it eagerly, tucking it into his Speedos. Then he turned and began jogging away before checking himself. Glancing back, he said with a grin, "Take it easy, *Peregrino*."

Peregrino? Diego mused. *Maybe I was a pilgrim once.* He watched the boy dashing towards the bridge before he lost sight of him among the crowds, and briefly his mind cast back to those easy rhythm days of his childhood and his playground of the fields and rivers. *I've conquered the stage, but never myself*, Diego thought bitterly as he turned on his heels and followed the promenade in the direction of Nessie.

Past the restaurants, the paving narrowed, trailing the main road. On the shelter of a tram stop, Diego noticed a poster advertising his concert in the city. His image was stoic and showed him looking up towards the heavens. Streaking from his Stratocaster guitar was a lightning bolt. Diego grimaced and turned his gaze away to face the river. He stared blankly across the green water, his eyes following the bending ripples; breathing deeply, he fingered his wedding ring. Then he pulled out his cigarette case and ran a finger across its silver surface. He considered smoking to calm himself but found himself dropping the case over the railings and into the water below instead. He didn't watch it sink; instead, he tipped his hat further over his eyes and resumed walking.

Soon he spotted parasols outside a bar across the street in a small plaza. A barman with his arms folded was standing in the doorway, staring past his empty tables and an olive tree to the widening river. Nessie wasn't there, nevertheless, Diego went inside. He bought himself a packet of cigarettes and ordered a whisky, which he drank at the bar counter in one long slug. He left and pressed on towards a suspension bridge. The sun was now nudging westward, casting thick shadows from the concrete pillars of the bridge. Diego passed under it, and before too long, the city disappeared behind cliffs.

After a time, he could taste salt in the air and, further, along the estuary, he saw a beach and a port. Drawing nearer, he eyed sunbathers gathered around a lifeguard tent and a beach café. Stopping to take in the scene and turning towards the sea, Diego spotted a girl in a sun hat standing at the shoreline. Behind her on the beach was a lavender backpack propped up in the sand next to a pair of walking shoes. It was Nessie. Diego jumped down from the wall edging the sand. He dropped his pack and jacket beside hers, unlaced his boots and removed his sweat-stained socks. Beyond the port, the sea and the sky mixed into a pale blue on the horizon. Diego felt the urge to throw off his clothes and swim towards the nothingness, but instead he rolled his jeans above his shins and stepped into the sea beside Nessie.

She turned her head towards him, smiling casually. "How's it going?"

"So so. This seawater feels really good on my feet."

"It's like a painting," Nessie remarked, turning her attention to the horizon again.

"*Bonito*," replied Diego thoughtfully. "It'd be nice to share it with Mari." Immediately he felt foolish for that comment. Not because he didn't miss Mari, but because he wasn't sure where he was heading with Nessie.

"Mari, that's your wife?"

Diego felt the current dragging at his ankles. "Um, yes, but things are a bit tricky between us at the moment."

"Oh, sorry about that." Feeling awkward Nessie resolved to change the subject and said, "So what made you walk your last Camino?"

Diego contrived a smile. "You're very kind changing the subject like that, but your question is kind of related. I met

Mari in Madrid, and you might say she was the catalyst to my walking the second leg of my Camino." He laughed mockingly at himself. "Another time I almost blew it with her!"

Nessie felt her cheeks reddening. "I can't believe it, I'm always putting my foot in it like that!"

"That's okay, how were you to know? I haven't exactly told you much about myself. You're the one who was brave enough to tell me about your boyfriend. So let's even things up. How about I tell you about my Camino and Mari?"

"You're sure?"

"Yes. I get the feeling you're an honest Welsh girl. I think I can trust you with my story."

"I thank you for your confidence, kind sir. I won't divulge your secrets nor judge your sins – even at the burning stake!"

"Fancy a smoke?"

"Lush."

They were both laughing and smoking by the sea as Diego began his story.

5

HOPE

"I walked to Santiago from my village in northern Spain, some five hundred kilometres away, along the most popular Camino path, the Camino Francés. On the way, I discovered what I wanted to do with the rest of my life – to play the flamenco guitar.

"My dream took me to Madrid, where I met Mari in a flamenco bar – she's a dancer. Somehow, and to this day, I still don't know how I did it, we eventually hooked up.

"But almost immediately, I did my best to screw things up. One evening after failing an audition as a lead guitarist for a flamenco show, I rocked up half-cut at the club, a *tablao*, where Mari was dancing. Long story short, I got my butt kicked out of the club and onto the street. The next day I left Madrid with my tail between my legs, and my travels led me towards Andalucía. But after getting off a bus at the wrong station and taking several wrong turns, I found myself on another Camino path – the Camino Mozarábe. I had no choice but to go on; hope remained as long as I had my music and kept walking.

"It was late summer when I returned to Madrid. The city was still scorching, but everything felt different and second chances felt possible. I showed up at a flamenco school I had been too chicken-shit to enter when I was previously in the city. To my surprise, they found some endowment money, and I was in. Every day I expected them to tell me to hit the road. But they didn't! And with things going well, I found the courage to contact Mari again.

"So, one night I waited for her outside the flamenco tablao, hoping to catch her after the show. I was petrified. Half of me wanted to get out of there and do what I used to do in those old streets – busk and hang out. I felt the urge to drink, laugh, smoke a joint. To enjoy the late summer night and damn tomorrow. Though the other side of me had found resilience to my weaknesses; perhaps it was the routine of studying the guitar at the music school, I'm not sure. But I thought, I can't play that game anymore. Not if I wanted to play the guitar at the level I knew I could, not if I wanted to be anything more than a half-remembered street musician and a good-time guy.

"Waiting, I saw a sliver of the moon through the gaps between the rooftops. Somehow it seemed to calm me, and I continued to wait, trying to figure out what I might say to Mari. But someone was looking down on me that night because instead of her telling me to piss off, she agreed to meet me the next day."

Diego took a final drag on his cigarette and turned his head away from the horizon. "I'm hungry. Let's see if there's anywhere to eat seafood?"

Nessie grinned. "Sea monsters love sea food."

They collected their things from the sand and strolled up the beach towards the port.

6

SEAFOOD

"*Peregrinos*, if you're hungry grab a table. Lunch ends at two," urged the young waiter as they entered the indoor fish market. The man had sharp features enhanced by an equally sharp goatee.

The pungent, sweet aroma of the ocean, and the crisp sounds of ice being packed around fish, swept around them as they eagerly followed the waiter through the market. Outside a restaurant, the waiter waved his hand across the tables inviting them to select one; he reminded Diego of a matador. Small-framed, yet muscular, he carried himself with the self-assuredness of someone used to dealing with life's hazards. They selected a table beside some of the staff, now eating and when they were settled the waiter handed Diego the wine menu.

Nessie glanced at the chalkboard listing the *menu do dia* and asked the waiter in English if there was also a regular menu.

"*Senhora*," he replied, gesturing across to the fish stalls. "We have a very wide menu; let's go and see what's left."

He led them across to a stall where a squat woman with bushy brown hair and a contented smile was scrubbing down a stainless-steel work surface. There was a bewildering choice of fish. But with some guidance from the woman and the waiter, Diego and Nessie settled on lemon sole. Diego was excited, especially as it reminded him of a time in London when he had enjoyed the same fish in a Soho restaurant, not far from the recording studio where he'd been working on his first album.

The waiter's assertiveness resumed at the table and he sold Diego an expensive bottle of sweet white wine. Shortly afterwards another waiter arrived with their now grilled fish. Diego and Nessie made small talk as they ate. Though, as the fish and wine warmed Diego's mood, he began to feel hopeful that all was not lost with Mari. *You still love me and I love you*, he thought. So after a while, he looked up from his plate and said to Nessie, "Things moved fast after I met Mari the next day."

"They did?"

Diego grinned. "I was beginning to clean up my act – I'd had a haircut and a shave."

Nessie's eyebrows drew together and she said, "And when you met she immediately noticed, right?"

Diego nodded. "She did; as soon as we met at Madrid's central park, El Retiro. We idled along several paths and our conversation was easy. I told her about my Mozarábe Camino in Andalucía. To my relief, she didn't hold any grudges about my stupidity at her show; it was all water under the bridge as far as she was concerned. Then she opened up to me, saying she was seriously considering giving up her life as a dancer as she wanted to try other creative things.

"We continued to walk and talk, oblivious to everything apart from our conversation, and later we found ourselves outside a lakeside café. We ate lunch there, paid for by Mari I might add – I only had a few Euros to my name at the time. And I told her about my first few weeks back in Madrid and my plans."

Diego went on to explain that he'd got a barman's job at a *taberna* in the centre of Madrid, a place where he'd once enquired at before, Casa Cerveza. He had worked there in the evenings and attended the flamenco school during the day. Diego smiled as he remembered how out of place he had initially felt there. "They made me take classes with kids learning the rules of music and I had to pass certain grades. Definitely not my thing! Luckily, though, I had separate classes with Francis, my maestro, who had a lot of mileage under his fingers and didn't care too much for music sheets, but he did make me practice for hours on end. He was one of those guys who don't say much when you ask them a question. He just used to close his eyes and repeat: '*Práctica, práctica…*' I reckon he was a little deaf."

Nessie laughed. "Sounds like Francis was a character, alright."

"He was, but I'm doing him a bit of a disservice; actually he was very open to experimenting with the guitar. I could see that when he played. You might say he was married to the guitar, but not bound by its rules."

Nessie put her fork down and thought for a moment. "Is that how you see marriage? A union not bound by rules?"

Diego wasn't sure if Nessie was flirting with him and sounding him out, or being more serious. Eventually, he responded, "Guess it depends on whom you marry." Slightly defensively he added, "It's only more recently that my relationship with Mari has struggled. For much of the time, it had felt like that afternoon at the park. Mari sitting across from me, her arm stretched across the table and her hand fitting smoothly into mine, like the lacquered neck of a Spanish guitar."

"That's very poetic, Diego."

"Well, I have written the odd lyric or two."

"I guess the rest is history, as they say?"

"Something like that. I worked hard at the music school

and practised the guitar any spare moment I got. And there were opportunities to perform on Casa Cerveza's tiny stage. Sometimes Mari would join me at the bar after her shows and I'd walk her home and stay over. Before long, staying over became a permanent thing. Now I was helping with the bills, Mari felt comfortable not committing to all of the flamenco gigs that came her way, and she dabbled in other arts such as painting and photography. Later, occasionally, I was offered paid work at some of the city's flamenco tablaos. Furthermore, I was drawing quite a crowd when I performed at Casa Cerveza. Then one night, when I was playing, a music man strolled through the doors of the *taberna*.

Nessie wiped her lips with her napkin. "That man was Mark?"

Diego gestured with his wine glass, before taking a sip. "Well guessed. I can still remember his first words to me: 'You can carry on working like a dog and practising your elegant finger picking, but the reality is no one cares. Millionaire pop artists pack football stadiums with little more than a synthesiser and four chords.'

"It was hard to argue with his point, especially as I'd started to feel restless and frustrated with Francis' repetitive training drills. Before I knew it, I'd quit the flamenco school and cut a track with Marco. Although that first record retained some authenticity, it failed in the charts. But that didn't deter him; soon after rock and rap found their way into my music and I had a number one hit in the Spanish charts. A tried and tested formula, really – modernising a music genre and putting it in front of a new generation."

Diego reached for the wine bottle and tilted it towards Nessie's empty glass, although she shook her head. Instead, he proceeded to pour the remains into his own glass and then drained it in one long swallow. His eyes dwelled on the empty bottle, weighing up the merits of drinking some more wine. But noticing Nessie trying to catch the eye of their waiter, who was now having lunch with the rest of the staff, he surmised they'd better resume walking.

Diego looked over at him. *"Señor, la cuenta."* The waiter nodded back, and Diego stood up and removed his wallet from a pocket.

"Let me pay too," urged Nessie.

Diego shook his head firmly. "No, it's on me. Especially as I treated you like my shrink, or something."

Nessie winked. "Okay, that's your session over then. *Gracias* for lunch."

Diego grinned. *"Croeso."* Nessie raised her eyebrows in astonishment at hearing 'you're welcome' in her native tongue. As Diego paid the waiter he explained, "I get around... I once met Tom Jones at a festival, where I picked up a word or two from him."

"I bet you picked up more than a word or two with him... So I guess that means I have to sleep with you now," said Nessie, matching Diego's grin. It was Diego's turn to raise his eyebrows. She added, "I get around too."

7

BETWEEN TWO WATERS

The sun had wheeled westwards, and they noticed a yellow Camino arrow pointing towards a bridge spanning the harbour. They repositioned their hats, stopping at the steps to the bridge as Nessie fingered through her guidebook.

She looked up at Diego and said, "Vila do Conde sounds nice, plus it has plenty of accommodation options, including a pilgrim *albergue*."

"How far is it?"

"About twenty kilometres."

"Quite a hike in this heat," remarked Diego glancing up at the sun.

"Yeah, but I need to keep the KMs up."

Maybe you should make your boyfriend wait, thought Diego, as he discovered himself feeling jealous of him. It was a strange sensation given that only moments before he'd been thinking how he still loved Mari. But in his forlorn state he wanted to feel the assurance of love. He replied, "Okay, but it could be late by the time we arrive."

"I could reserve a place," she responded, glancing back at the guide. "Let's see… perhaps one of the private hostels?"

"Maybe we should get something a little more comfortable… after the first day of walking." Diego adjusted his stance and added as casually as he could muster, "A nice double room, perhaps?"

Nessie looked up from the book, her eyes flickering as she thought. "Aren't pilgrims meant to rough it a bit?"

Diego scowled inwardly as he realised how easily he'd just returned to his old womanising self. He stepped back slightly and laughed awkwardly. "Perhaps you're right, I don't want to be responsible for you missing out on the authentic pilgrim experience."

"I'm sorry," said Nessie. "I didn't mean to give you the wrong impression back at the restaurant. I don't know what I'm thinking at the moment…"

Diego nodded tensely and said, "No, I should say sorry – my mistake." He diverted his eyes up to the bridge. "But if we stand any chance of getting a hostel, or any accommodation at all tonight, we'd better put some distance between ourselves and here."

"Agreed," replied Nessie. She returned the guidebook to her pack and began climbing the steps. Diego followed behind her. Reaching the top he felt Nessie's paces vibrating through the metal walkway and she was already a third of the way across the bridge. On the other side, she slowed down to accommodate him and asked, "How long have you been married?"

Diego paused, then finally replied. "It'll be five years in September."

"Gosh, your anniversary isn't far away."

"No, it's not," muttered Diego.

"Sorry, there I go again. I don't mean to pry."

"It's okay, there's no hiding the fact my marriage might be on the rocks."

"It's worth fighting for, no?"

"I believe so," Diego answered. "We've had some amazing

times together." He half-smiled. "And our wedding and honeymoon remain the best days of my life." He cocked his head towards the sea, gulping in the air. "We were married in a seaside villa in a swanky part of Marbella, Puerto Banús, then honeymooned in Paris." He paused, remembering Mari had bought him the cigarette case from an antique store on the honeymoon as a wedding gift. His smile evaporated into a frown and he sighed. "Life was sweet for a few years."

They began walking and shortly Nessie said, "It's funny. You know, I can't really place when my relationship with Michael, my boyfriend, started. He always seemed to be around. We grew up in the same street and played together as kids. Then one day, as teenagers I think, we just decided we were boyfriend and girlfriend."

"Guess that's pretty common – I've seen that with a lot of my friends. Good to have a soul mate, though?"

"I always thought that, and I feel comfortable with Michael. We know everything about each other. But I'm not sure if that's enough anymore? I've never dated anyone else, and I have so many ideas of things I want to do."

"You've never dated anyone else, but you say you get around?"

"I must have made myself sound like a right slut? Well… I exaggerated a bit – I snogged a couple of guys once when I was drunk at my work Christmas party. And I did meet this fella, well another colleague, for a drink just before I came away here. I actually considered sleeping with him."

"Well, you have much stronger morals than I do." Diego glanced at the sea. "Back in the day, you could have described me as a slut. I had a bit of a reputation. I've been faithful to Mari, but I have to admit there have been one or two times I've been tempted to sleep with someone else. There's always been a lot of girls hanging around the shows and the parties, especially in the early days when I was this new flamenco kid on the block."

"Really? You never did sleep with any of them?"

"No, but maybe I should have… I'm getting the impression that Michael is the faithful type?"

"Absolutely. Everyone seems to think he's great, and my parents adore him."

"But what do you think?"

"I know he really cares for me, but sometimes I don't feel I care about him the same way." Nessie stopped abruptly. "Now I think he's going to propose to me when he meets me in Spain. He started hinting at marriage, soon as I mentioned I was going to do this walk."

"Hmm, and you don't know how you'll respond?"

"No, not at all. I feel like I'm in a terrible predicament!"

"Well, wish I knew what to say." Diego forced a grin. "But I'm not the best person to be giving any advice on the prospect of marriage at the moment."

They resumed walking, pacing in silence and consumed by their thoughts. Only speaking occasionally to pass a remark about the landscape or sights. They passed a small chapel on a rocky promontory and stopped at a standing stone with an inscription. Diego translated the words: *A pen creates but also destroys nature.*

Nessie walked ahead and a series of uninterrupted boardwalks took them along beaches, through sand dunes and eventually to a fishing village. Lobster pots were stacked high along the promenade, and blue shacks storing fishing equipment also served as dens for tanned fishermen playing cards. Diego lingered. His skin was oozing with booze and his shirt was sticking to his back. He removed his pack and sat on a seawall. When Nessie noted Diego had stopped she turned around and joined him.

As much as he didn't want to be alone, Diego said, "I'm done for today."

"I don't think it's too far?" Nessie replied, reaching around her pack for her guidebook.

Diego sighed. "I really do need to rest."

Nessie wasn't ready to be alone either. She sat on the wall and grabbed a couple of Kendal Mint Cake bars and handed one to Diego. Chewing on her bar, Nessie opened her book and looked at its map. "Vila do Conde is only about five kilometres further. Are you sure you can't make that?"

"I wish I could, but I need to get out of these boots too. Let's stay here for the night... and we can make an early start of it tomorrow?"

Nessie sighed deeply and fidgeted with her hat. "I just can't. Does that make me pathetic?"

"Of course not, if you're feeling the need to keep going today you should."

"Yes, I think I should. I owe it to Michael to be there on time – now that I've agreed to meet him. Hopefully, by then I'll be able to talk to him. You know... speak to him about the future."

Nessie washed her bar down with some water and put her book away. Then she got up from the wall. "Well, Mr Lightning, it was good meeting you."

Diego stood up. "*¡Buen camino!*"

"What's that mean?"

"It's a common phrase people use a lot on the Camino when they greet each other. It translates as 'good way', but I've just remembered its deeper meaning. It's an acknowledgement that a pilgrim is seeking their best life, their true reason for being. Whomever I met along the pilgrim roads understood that."

Nessie digested his words, then said, "Thanks for being so lush, Diego."

He shrugged his shoulders. "*¡Gracias!*"

"Well, *Buen camino.*"

Diego smiled. "*Buen camino*, Nessie."

"I wonder if Michael will start saying *buen camino* too?" said Nessie.

"I hope he does."

"Guess I'll find out soon enough."

Diego tapped the brim of his hat. "Guess you will."

They hugged, gripping each other hard, feeling the other's heart beating. Neither felt like letting go, although feeling the breeze through her hair Nessie eventually stood back.

Nessie smiled and said, "I'm sorry. It's just that I'm not quite ready for sex, drugs and rock 'n' roll." Her smile twisted into a smirk, and she added, "But give me your number. Maybe I will be tomorrow."

Diego winked. "Well, see you further down the road in that case!"

He retrieved his phone from a pocket. Its screen displayed a series of missed calls and messages; glancing at them quickly established that none were from Mari. They exchanged numbers, and then Diego sat back on the wall while Nessie shouldered her pack. Diego gave her the rock-on-hand sign as they separated. She returned it with the finger gun hand sign, before she reached back into her bag and tossed Diego another Kendal Mint Cake bar.

She grinned. "The Mint Cakes are on me, cowboy."

Diego smiled back at Nessie and she resumed walking along the promenade. He continued watching her until she removed her shoes and socks, skipped onto the beach and was out of sight amongst the wooden fishing vessels nestling in the sand.

Diego continued to sit on the wall. He ate a Mint Cake, flicked vaguely through his phone messages, and speculated if this fishing village would be the end of his walk. Wondered if he'd see Mari for their anniversary. He turned to face the sea and his eyes followed the seagulls riding high on the thermals. His nostrils widened as the aroma of barbequing mackerel from one of the shacks wafted in his direction. His shoulders ached, and he realised he was in the mood for a *cerveza*. Diego switched off his phone, got up from the wall and decided to seek out a bed for the night in the village.

8

BESIDE THE SEA

The main street ran behind the promenade and in a restaurant, Diego asked about accommodation. An ageing woman with sandy hair gestured to her husband, who was quietly sitting, his head angled up at the news on the television set mounted in a corner above the bar. His weather-beaten face bore endurance and the remains of his silver hair tangled around the sides of his head like a fraying fishing net. He rose and pointed a thick thumb through the window and down the street.

When Diego saw the faded quilt with floral patterns covering the bed and noticed the shabby shower curtain in the bathroom, his immediate reaction was to leave. However, he tempered his thoughts as soon as the elderly man handed him the key and mentioned there was no need for any paper-work or to pay in advance. Diego should find him in his restaurant when he was ready to check out. The feeling of anonymity, as well as having the man's trust, suddenly made the place more appealing. As soon as the proprietor left, Diego stripped off and pulled back the shower curtain.

The sun was half-submerged in the sea when Diego

arrived at the modest beach bar and ordered himself a large beer. A jovial group of middle-aged couples occupied the largest table on the wooden planked terrace. Diego pulled out a chair on the perimeter, giving himself a good view of the bay. He casually ran a hand through his drying hair and pushed it back over his crown, before tying it into a ponytail. Then he lit himself a cigarette.

Watching the sun melting away, he wondered where Mari might be and what she was up to. He reached into a pocket of his jeans for his phone and switched it on. A stream of messages from Mark lit up its screen, and there was an overwhelming number of notifications on his social media apps. He glanced at a couple of them on his Facebook fan page, discovering that many of his followers were ruthless in their condemnation of his stage walk-off. However, some wished him a speedy recovery from his 'exhaustion', though most were relieved his tour wasn't cancelled – just postponed. Diego smirked and took a sip of beer, thinking, *Perhaps Marco could add dehydration into the excuses mix!* He rechecked his messages though he still couldn't see one from Mari.

He turned the phone back off and gazed across at the sun's halo burning faintly like the last embers of a fire, the light rolling its way across the waves like a ruffled red carpet. It felt like a pathway to America – which was the next stage of Mark's big plans for him. Again Diego began to doubt his actions. *Is it too late? Have I already burned that bridge?* He swallowed another mouthful of beer as he searched for answers on the amber horizon. But nothing came to him, and he signalled the barman for another.

The first pale stars appeared above the dark sea, and its waters sighed as they sucked up the beach. Diego felt the urge to drink some more, but just clenching his glass felt arduous. Moreover, the idea of walking any further filled him with dread. Although he was only thirty, he began to wonder whether his excesses might finally be catching up with him. Had the feather of his youth blown away for good? He removed his sleeping pills from his pocket and washed some down his throat with the remains of his beer, then he rose from his chair and trudged back to the guesthouse.

Diego awoke to the sound of whistling winds and crashing waves. He looked up at the ceiling fan, not wanting to move, his eyes fixated on the circular trajectory of the wooden blades. Had he imagined the figure of Francis or had it been his father beneath the exit sign at the concert? Was he losing it? He felt sick to his stomach. Not helped by his throbbing head. But he was most upset by the situation with Mari, and he felt a great longing to see her. He stayed in bed all morning, only rising to use the toilet and to check his phone to see if she had messaged him. She hadn't, but Mark continued to chase him, leaving several messages – each one increasingly irate. By the evening, his sore head had faded to a manageable ache, and his stomach had settled, so he left the room, not caring to check his appearance, though aware of the stubble now prickling his face.

He stepped outside into a thin light, a veil of fog drifting across the beach and masking the sea. A barrel-shaped lighthouse made of concrete, not much taller than a telephone box, blinked a red light from the promenade. Diego stopped beside it and turned to face the wind. With the damp air sweeping across him, the moment brought to mind his near-death experience. The time he'd got caught up in the narrow gorge and the flash flood on his southerly Camino path in Andalucía. He'd sensed a benign feeling of acceptance during those apparent final moments of life. *The sea will keep,* he said to himself as he became aware of the aromas of barbequing fish. He smiled sardonically and wandered in the direction of the restaurant.

When he reached it the elderly man with tangled hair was

around the side of the building standing over a simple barbeque. He fanned the smoking charcoal and cooking mackerel with a side of cardboard torn from a Super Bock beer box. His quiet contentment reminded Diego of how his papá had once worked his candyfloss machine in the plaza of their village. It didn't go unnoticed that the man's tubby and stocky stature was not unlike his father's shape. Sensing Diego's presence, the man looked up and smiled.

"Smells amazing," said Diego, his mood lifting a little.

"Are you hungry?"

"Famished!"

"You like seafood?" Diego nodded enthusiastically. The man reached down to a bucket of water and pulled out a handful of clams and rinsed them before setting them across his grill. "Go inside, and my wife will find you a table," he said without looking back up.

Diego brushed aside the beaded curtain and entered the restaurant. Fishermen wearing thick shirts and rubber boots were sitting at the bar. Serving them behind the counter was the man's wife. Towards the entrance and sitting at one of the Formica tables were two middle-aged women. They'd hung their waterproof jackets on the back of their chairs and Diego figured they were both pilgrims passing through. Upon noticing Diego, the wife approached him and, with little fuss, pulled out a small table and sat him in a corner beside the ice cream fridge. Diego accepted the wife's offer of the *menu do dia*; it didn't require an explanation.

Nor did he enquire about the choice of *tinto*. But when the smiling, chubby-faced waitress delivered his half-litre carafe, he wasn't dissatisfied with the house red wine, thinking it tasted *fiable*, dependable. Waiting for his supper, he observed the comings and goings of the place. The wife delivering plates of seafood from her husband's grill and routinely filling glasses at the Super Bock beer tap. Elderly men coming in to drink an espresso or something stronger, often settling at a table to read the evening newspapers. Some joined the domino game, but never did anyone at that table raise their voice, nor bang a domino down hard on the table. Others came in to scrape a lottery card or buy cigarettes, often lingering to chat.

He also took in the décor. On the walls were framed photos of the villagers through the eras, as well as landscape shots taken across the seasons. There were cactuses on the shelves, and on the chequered tiled floor were larger plant pots mixed with thistles and colourful flowers, similar to the ones scattered across the dunes. He also spotted a couple of Camino scallop shells strung up on a wall. Diego, himself, wasn't unnoticed but nobody seemed to recognise him or, if they did, didn't care to give him ideas of grandeur.

By the time Diego's seafood arrived he'd already drunk more than half of his wine and felt more content with his present circumstances. He didn't want to return to his room, so after devouring his food, he ordered more wine and hung around until after the last customers had left, then he got up from his table and moved to the bar. The husband was wearing his reading glasses and holding a lengthy till receipt up to the light. His wife and the cheery waitress were cleaning up in the adjoining kitchen.

"A good evening?" enquired Diego.

The man lowered his glasses and looked up. "I can't complain."

"I once worked in a bar. Probably the best job I ever had."

The man smiled nostalgically. "I was once a fisherman… that was the best job I ever had." He reached a hand across the bar. "My name is Remigio."

Shaking Remigio's hand Diego replied, "*Mucho gusto.* I'm Diego." Feeling the old man's coarse hand, Diego imagined the man rowing out to sea, beyond the fog and the bay, perhaps beyond his limits. He looked up and asked, "Why did you give up?"

Remigio pulled his hand back and began massaging it with his thumb. "As soon as they took the fun out of fishing… it was time to do something else."

"What do you mean?"

"Commercial fishing and the large modern trawlers."

Diego nodded understandingly. "Ah, *claro*. So you moved into hospitality."

"I figured people would always eat fish." The old man put his glasses down and winked. "It's the catching them that's changed."

Diego raised his wine glass at Remigio, feeling he was a person who might understand his own story. Equally, Remigio sensed Diego's need to talk and, being a good listener, he reached for a bottle of honey-coloured wine from the bar fridge and poured himself a glass.

Remigio subtly looked Diego up and down, before he pulled out a stool and asked, "You're walking the Camino?"

"Ha, I don't much look like a pilgrim, do I? Man, I'm not sure I look like anything these days!"

Remigio took a sip of his wine. "This restaurant has taught me a lot about people, and fundamentally people don't change. It's just the changing circumstances of their lives that give them the impression of being off-course inside."

"Hmm," muttered Diego thinking of Arnau. "That's the sort of thing the owner of my local bar would have said, the place I once worked as a teenager. Your place reminds me a lot of there. It's quite ironic, it was called Bar Paradiso, but I had a love, hate relationship with that place – and my village."

"It's in the north of Spain?"

"You're good."

"Well, perhaps the name was taken from the surrounding countryside. I'm told the Camino Francés is a walkers' paradise, for example."

Diego shrugged his shoulders. "I never thought about it

that way. But actually, the Camino passes through my village and it was eventually my old man who gave me the push I needed to leave, so I ended up walking the Camino to Santiago. And here I am again, contemplating my life on this Portuguese Camino. But even back then I had a sense of who I was. I just didn't know what I wanted to do with my life at the time. I was a country boy, and I've gone on to be a married man, even a rock star."

At that point Remigio adjusted his stool a little closer towards Diego, so he didn't miss a word. Knowing he had the man's full attention Diego asked, "How hard was it for you to start over?"

After a thoughtful sip of his wine, Remigio said, "Once I'd realised I'd learned as much as I could from the sea, the decision to start afresh was easy for me."

"*¿Qué?*" Diego scratched his chin. "You learned something from the sea?"

"To fully understand, you would have to spend time on the water. Then you would know it, that truth."

After several sips of wine and a moment of silence, Diego said, "Truth?"

"You can only find out this for yourself, or maybe you already know? After all, you must have walked beside many rivers."

Remigio's wife came out of the kitchen and the staff left the restaurant. Remigio rose from his stool. "It's late. I need my sleep."

Diego placed his wine glass on the bar and slipped off his stool. Then he nodded at Remigio and his wife saying, "*Buenas noches,*" as he turned to face the door.

The fog had now encroached to the edge of the promenade and the fishing boats pulled up at the beach were faint smudges, though the lighthouse pulsed brightly through the gloom. Diego walked leisurely with his hands in his trouser pockets and was soon at the guesthouse. Entering his room, he switched the fan off and opened the window then pulled his boots off and stretched himself across the bed, tucking a pillow behind his head. Resting his eyes, Diego listened to the waves fizzing onto the shore.

As the sea receded and murmured beyond the shoreline, Diego sensed his breath – steady and calm – and in that tranquil moment, a voice from inside spoke up and said: *trust the path*. He understood he should continue walking this new path to see where it took him, that wallowing in indecision would get him nowhere. Likewise, he was curious to discover this 'truth' Remigio had hinted at. He sat up straight, swivelled off the bed and searched around in his pockets for his sleeping pills. Though, as soon as he found them he lost the urge to take any, and he dropped them into his pack. Instead, he removed his clothes, pulled out his sleeping bag and unrolled it across the bed before collapsing into a deep sleep.

Morning soon came, and Diego hastily got himself together. It was still early and though the thick fog had cleared, strands of mist still hung around the fishing boats. Entering the restaurant, it felt as if it hadn't closed for the night; it was full of fishermen who had swept through its doors on the dawn tide and they occupied most of the tables. Remigio's wife was attending to them and Remigio was at the bar filling glasses with an assortment of colourful liquors. Diego felt tempted to join the fishermen in their morning ritual and try one of the drinks. However, the aroma of ground coffee and the clatter of metal on ceramic alerted him to the need for a decent breakfast. Remigio nodded at Diego and gestured at a free stool at the counter.

Diego took his spot at the bar and noticed the difference from the evening before. Till receipts and sugar sachets already speckled the floor and individuals were figuring out what the day's news meant for them. Some farmers standing around the counter gazed up at the weather forecast on the television, whilst elderly men rhythmically stirred their coffees, heads bent over their morning papers. Amongst them all, Diego's life felt much simpler. Shortly, another barman, youthful and tanned, took Diego's order of fried eggs served over potatoes and ham, with a *café solo*, black coffee to drink.

After breakfast and at the point of returning the key, Remigio refused payment for Diego's meals, simply stating they were both pilgrims, and pilgrims found a way of giving back to the other. Though Diego insisted on paying for his room and his wine – he didn't expect anyone to pay for his indulgences.

They parted with a firm handshake and benevolent smiles. Outside, back at the promenade, Diego noticed on the base of the seawall a yellow Camino arrow. It was painted with three simple brushstrokes and pointed north, along the coast. Diego stepped across to the wall, sat down on it and faced the sea and the thinning mist. He took a deep breath, retrieved his phone from a pocket and switched it on. Then he typed out a text:

Marco, perhaps some sort of formal notice will be needed… but for the sake of getting to the point – YOU'RE FIRED.

Diego paused to think what else he might need to say, but he didn't hesitate any longer in pressing the send button. He looked up and squinted as he gazed at the misty scene ahead of him. Then he composed a follow-up message to Mark:

To save us all time and money for my breach of contract, I'm willing to give you 100% of my future royalties. All I ask is you arrange for the best publicist at the label to put out a statement stating the tour has been cancelled: INDEFINITELY. And to offer my sincerest apologies to the fans. You can liaise with me through Gracia.

Diego turned off the phone and gripped it hard, his attention grabbed by the sounds of waves crashing over a reef. Then he discovered himself dropping off the wall onto the beach and walking through the ribbons of mist towards the shoreline. Arriving at the water's edge, Diego pulled his arm back. Then as he flung his mobile into the applauding breakers he cried out above the groupie-shrieks of the gulls, "*Adiós*, phoney!"

A minute later, he lit himself a cigarette. Already the day was brightening, and the sea was turning cobalt blue.

9

BLUE MOON

D iego's boots crunched onto the sand blown across the promenade. He pulled on his pack and adjusted his Stetson. He glanced along the bay and his northern path, and savouring the moment believed it might taste even better with some whisky. He reached inside his jacket and had a nip from his hip flask.

The Camino path led away from the village and the bay, joining a rural road cutting through a pine and eucalyptus forest. Later, the road came to a roundabout, where a café next to it caught Diego's attention. There were several people inside – they had that familiar locals' way about them. Different opinions, although quietly accepting of each other. Diego ordered himself a coffee but didn't linger inside, instead going out to the patio and a table that looked onto the road. He sat down, glanced over his shoulder and added some whisky to his coffee, then he pulled the brim of his hat further down, so that it shaded his eyes, and peeked up at the late August sun. It was high above the luscious forest and the sea beyond. Winding out the table's parasol, he stretched his legs onto the opposite chair and lit himself a cigarette. Observing a tractor dealership on the other side of the road, he briefly thought of home, as he remembered his first job at the local dealership there. It had been a brief affair, just half a day, before he'd taken off to see Arnau about the bar job he'd always promised him.

His musings were distracted by the beats of salsa music. A youthful man emerged from the wooded road. Upon spotting Diego, he gave him the thumbs-up. The man was carrying a rucksack, wearing a tight navy sweatshirt and faded jeans. He approached Diego, his music growing in volume.

"Alright, mate! You walking the Camino too?" he asked in a London accent, removing his pack and placing it on a chair at Diego's table.

"*¿Qué?*" whispered Diego, pretending he didn't understand.

"Ah, *lo siento* mate," replied the man switching to Spanish. "You're Spanish, guess you don't understand English?"

Diego looked up and imitating Mark's exaggerated English accent offered, "I'm not sure I understand you English, although I understand your language well enough."

The man grinned. "Well, I beg your pardon, sir! And I agree, I don't understand my countrymen either. Most of them right up their arses."

Caught off guard, Diego found his dimples pulling the corners of his mouth into a little smile. He looked the Englishman over. He had a pale complexion and his reddish-brown hair was cropped. Diego also noticed the man's left eye occasionally twitched. He guessed the man was similar in age to himself, perhaps in his early thirties.

"You got a spare smoke?"

Diego nodded and pulled out his cigarettes from a pocket.

"Cheers, mate!" he said, helping himself to one. "I'm gonna enjoy this. I'm giving up when I get to Santiago."

Diego lit the man's cigarette and after a satisfying drag the man asked, "How's the coffee?"

"Adequate."

"That's good enough for me, mate. Fancy another one?"

"Why not," replied Diego. "And could you do me a favour and turn your music down a bit?"

"Oh, yeah. Sorry," he responded, reaching over to a side pocket on his pack. He pulled out a small cube-shaped speaker and switched it off.

"Bluetooth?" asked Diego.

He nodded, then asked, "*¿Café con leche?*"

"*Perfecto.*"

The man spun around, dropping a shoulder, almost as if he was about to perform a salsa move, and light-footed it towards the café's entrance. Diego shook his head slightly, thinking he'd only just shaken off Mark and suddenly was in the company of another Brit. And this one was definitely a poor substitute for Nessie. The man soon returned with their coffees and, sitting down, he stretched a hand across the table. "I'm Dave, by the way."

Diego shook Dave's hand and replied, "Diego. And yes, I am walking the Camino."

"Where did you start?"

"Um… Porto."

"I started in Lisbon, having a cracking time. Cheapest holiday I've ever had!"

Diego laughed. "Never really thought of the Camino as a vacation. But I like that idea; I'm long overdue one."

"Well, you know what they say: all work and no play…"

"…Makes Jack a dull boy," interjected Diego.

"Exactly. St. James was no square."

"*¿Qué?* I thought we were talking about a Jack?"

Dave's eyes flickered with excitement. "Mate, Jack is the equivalent of James in French. So the Camino de Santiago is also known as the pilgrimage of Saint Jacques. And this year is one of the special Holy Years of the Compostela – often referred to as the Jacobean year. It's a year they completely absolve pilgrims of their sins. Figured I could have a really good time on the way, but all will be forgiven when I walk through the Holy Door of the cathedral!"

"I like your style, Dave."

Dave grinned. "Plenty of fit chicks walking it too."

"Guess so, but I'm married."

"You are?" replied Dave, his faint eyebrows rising. "What a shame." He leaned back into his seat and took a sip of coffee and continued, "Never have thought that!"

After a long drag on his cigarette, Diego asked, "Why?"

"You don't look the married type, mate."

"There's a type? It's down to love!" Diego stubbed out his cigarette into an ashtray, then suddenly jumped up from his chair and swung his backpack over his shoulder. "And I'm not your mate!" he added as he left the café and stomped off towards a road sloping downhill.

Within minutes Diego heard the beats of salsa again and glancing over his shoulder, he saw Dave striding towards him and waving at him. Getting closer he yelled, "Geezer… slow down. This road isn't part of the Camino."

Diego paused. "It isn't?"

"No," said Dave, arriving beside Diego and twisting his neck back up the hill. "There was a Camino sign at the round-about, pointing straight on."

"Oh!"

"Easily done, mate. You don't have any cigarettes left, do you?"

"Thought you were giving up?"

"Yep, but anything goes until I reach Santiago. Remember?"

"You English," said Diego. "Always changing the rules to suit yourselves." He offered Dave a cigarette before taking one himself. He lit them both and added, "Sorry I was a bit touchy at the café. I'm having marriage problems." Then he half-smiled and added a little ashamedly, "Mate."

"*No problemo*, figured as much," replied Dave as he turned on his heel to face uphill.

They strolled up the hill and stopped to finish their cigarettes beside the Camino sign mounted on a post, its arrow pointing towards a cobbled lane with a high grey wall and bright purple bougainvillaea trailing over it. Diego removed his jacket, Dave reduced the volume of his music, and they crossed over the roundabout. They dodged a couple of cowpats and found a comfortable walking rhythm together.

Shortly Diego asked, "You seem to know a lot about the history of the Camino, plus you speak Spanish?"

"Guess so."

"Care to elaborate?"

There was a slight edginess to Dave as he replied, "You know how it is: you pick a few things up here and there."

Diego turned his head around at Dave and in a more serious tone asked, "For example, where did you learn Spanish?"

Dave paused as he thought over the question, but relaxed as soon as he'd gathered his thoughts. "In London."

"That's where you're from?"

"Yep… Shepherd's Bush. I picked up Spanish at a salsa club near where I live. It's a decent club and there's a big Latino community in London, and they love to dance. A Colombian girl I know got me into salsa. Now it's kind of an addiction. And the Latino *chicas* are something else."

Diego grinned, and they resumed walking. "So you're planning on having a fiesta all the way to Santiago then."

"No reason why not to."

Diego nodded. "Guess not; still, I don't really get why you'd be walking it?"

"I don't look like the walking sort, no?"

"No more than me, I guess. But why the Camino in particular?"

"The Colombian woman I mentioned – she was kind of

my girl, wanted to settle down, and all that. Fun chick, but she's got a kid from a past relationship, and although the kid's great… I didn't want her to think I was her dad. So I got the heck out of Dodge and went to Lisbon. See the salsa scene is exploding there, and they mix it up with African beats too. I got myself a job as a driver at the docks for new cars arriving in the country. Shit work, but occasionally I got to deliver a car to a showroom around the country and that put the idea in my head to see some more. Got itchy feet, always have."

"You had a *chica* in Lisbon too?"

Dave smirked. "One or two."

Diego laughed.

Dave continued talking, "Anyway, I met this older Swiss geezer, a real gent, who was about to set off from Lisbon on the Camino. He's a widower but said he was ready to find love again. He figured any woman crazy enough to walk over 600 kilometres to Santiago might just be crazy enough to get involved with him. I thought, I can play that game too. I read a couple of books about the Camino and long story short – here I am."

Diego scratched the stubble under his chin. "But you're not seeking love?"

"Nah, mug's game that!"

"*¿Por qué…?* Why do you say that?"

Dave began thinking over his response, but a tractor rattling towards them diverted their attention. It passed them, and Dave reached into his pack. Retrieving his set of head-phones, he plugged himself into his phone and music. He pointed to his head yelling, "Mind if I listen to my music for a bit?" Diego eyed Dave curiously but responded by giving him a thumbs-up.

Dave's elongated shadow jigged along ahead and Diego was happy for him to set the pace. Eventually, the trail wound downhill, joining a tarmacked road before crossing a modern road bridge. Within minutes they were trailing beside its metal handrail and Diego was glancing down at the fast-flowing water below. His eyes traced its flowing circular patterns, reminding him of leaves swirling in the wind.

Soon after, his attention switched to Vila do Conde, the town on the opposite riverbank. He tapped Dave on the shoulder, who pulled his headphones away from his ears and glanced back. "My feet are aching from all those cobbles," Diego said, pointing across to the town. "Ready for lunch?"

"Sounds good."

On the other side, they headed through the town and to a row of restaurants on the riverbank. They settled at a table at a busy café with a wide terrace and Dave eagerly glanced around at the women having lunch. He also winked and nodded to a couple of walkers, whom Diego assumed he must have met at some point on his journey. It was a workers' café, but it also had a sign advertising the pilgrim menu of the day. Various groups of pilgrims were taking advantage. Dave removed his headphones and Diego reached for his cigarettes. After lighting a cigarette for them both, Diego turned his chair to face the river, drawn by the sound of the breeze hitting the masts of the boats. They clanked, groaned and whistled with stories.

"Lovely, eh?" said Dave breaking the tranquillity of the moment.

"What?"

"This place, the Camino. *¡Las chicas!*"

Diego exaggeratedly rotated his head around, then said sarcastically, "Ah, the girls, how could I have missed them!" Suddenly, however, he spotted a girl he did know. Sat alone at a table just inside the doorway of the café was the girl with the Candyfloss hair. Nessie. He jumped up and Dave's eyes curiously followed him as he strode inside.

Diego smiled as he looked down at Nessie at the table and said, "*¡Buen camino* señorita!*"

Nessie looked up. "So, you made it this far?"

"*Sí*, I have." He glanced at his boots and smirked as he said, "Even in my sissy shitkickers. But what are you doing here Nessie? I thought you'd be way ahead by now?"

Nessie placed her cutlery down on her plate and peeked into Diego's eyes. "Ner! Thought I'd take my time, you know. Get the full pilgrim experience, like you suggested. Michael will just have to wait for me in Tui, until I get there."

"Oh…? Well, we can't have you eating on your own." Diego nodded out through the door and towards Dave and their table. "I'm just out there with an English guy I've met. You'll join us?"

"Sure, that would be lush."

"I'll warn you, he sees himself as a bit of a Casanova."

Nessie grinned. "Well, I am a monster remember? Of the Welsh fire-breathing variety!"

Diego matched Nessie's grin for size as he replied, "Reckon you'll be fine then."

Nessie grabbed her backpack and arranged for a waiter to bring her food outside to their table, where Diego introduced her to Dave.

"Alright," said Dave shaking Nessie's hand. "How's it going?"

"Not bad, mate," replied Nessie. "Are you planning on walking all the way to Santiago?"

"I always go all the way." Diego ogled Dave sternly and he responded with a subtle wink before turning back towards Nessie. "Just joking. Yeah, that's the intention. But I'm in no rush to get there, don't want it to end. Having a banging time."

Nessie nodded. "I'm just starting to realise that."

"Well, stick around, we're only just getting going." Dave grinned at Diego. "Right *amigo*?"

"Perhaps," replied Diego. "Anyway, we should at least order some drinks to warm us up for this adventure. You drinking, Nessie?"

"Why not, I am on holiday after all. But I'll get them, I still owe you for that lunch, Diego. What would you fellas like?"

"A vodka and coke," replied Dave without a second thought.

Nessie smiled warmly at Diego. "A beer, right?" Before Diego had a chance to reply she'd already got up from the table and gone inside to find her waiter to order their drinks.

With Nessie away from their table Dave winked at Diego. "Mate, she's into you big time. I'd fill your boots."

"*¿Qué?* No way."

Dave leaned back in his chair and laughed. "I saw the way she looked at you and I couldn't miss the look you gave me when I was jesting with her." Diego shook his head. Dave's wrinkles stretched across his reddening forehead as his laughing became more mocking. "Don't be such a pussy, *hombre*. Perhaps you should get back on your horse and learn some new tricks?"

Diego reached for his cigarettes. "You ever been married, Dave?"

Dave's wrinkles creased further. "Come on! Look, I don't know the details of your situation, but I don't see your wife walking this Camino with you. Right now, it's just you here. Oh, and Nessie."

"You don't mince your words, do you?"

"I'm not built like that, Diego. Life's too short."

Nessie returned and they changed the conversation. Then moments later the waiter arrived with their drinks, including a beer for Nessie. She continued eating her meal and Diego and Dave both ordered hamburgers and fries. After they'd all finished eating, two Korean girls approached them. The small flags threaded on their backpacks were the giveaway, and Dave opted for the obvious question: "Girls – you're from South Korea?"

The girls giggled, and then the taller girl replied in English, "Yes, we're walking the Camino before we begin our careers back home." She turned her attention to Diego. "Are you Diego el Relámpago?"

He fidgeted and answered, "Sometimes." The girls smiled excitedly and grabbed their mobile phones, but Diego held his palms out. "But I'm just Diego today."

The Koreans looked puzzled but lowered their phones. The shorter girl murmured, "Sorry… you're very popular in Korea," she glanced at their packs resting against their table, "and it's crazy to find you walking the Camino too!"

"You're a music guy?" asked Dave.

Diego countered the question with a tight-lipped smile. Noticing Diego had lowered his hands and relaxed somewhat, Dave nodded at their table and said to the Koreans, "Pull up a chair and join us for a drink?" He added an earnest smile and the girls joined them at the table.

"What's your tipple?" asked Dave.

"Tipple?" said the taller girl.

"Drink, what do you like to drink?" explained Dave

"Ah, whisky," declared the taller girl.

Diego raised an arm in the air and gestured at the waiter. "Whisky it is, all round!" Almost immediately he found himself turning to Nessie. "That's okay with you – you like whisky?"

"Sure, but if I have one I won't be doing any walking today."

Diego grinned. "So fire water is the way to tame the Welsh dragon!" Nessie laughed and Diego said, "But we'd best make it doubles, just to be sure."

When the waiter returned with their drinks, Diego raised his glass and asked the Koreans their names. They learned the taller girl was called Ha-eun and Aera was the shorter girl. Next, he raised a glass and exclaimed, "*¡Buen camino!*" After they had all chinked their glasses Diego asked the girls, "So, flamenco, it's popular in Korea?"

They explained that Latin dances such as tango and salsa

had been popular in Korea for years, but more people were now getting into traditional Spanish music. Furthermore, and to Diego's surprise, his version of *Flamenco Nuevo* had a big following amongst a younger audience in Seoul, where the girls were from.

Everyone continued to chat into the afternoon and before long, paired off. Dave enthusiastically chatted about salsa music to the Koreans and Diego caught up with Nessie.

Nessie went to light herself a cigarette, but Diego beat her to it. "Let me," he said, leaning over with his lighter. "My turn."

"My turn?"

"Exactly. Remember, you lit mine when we first met at the railway station and you helped me get my swing back."

"Ah, yes. Some cigarette, that – you played with amazing style as soon as I lit it."

Nessie mentioning the cigarette reminded Diego that he'd subsequently dropped his silver cigarette case into the sea back in Porto. It had been a reckless action, yet he didn't feel regretful about throwing away the gift. Responding to Nessie he said, "Magic lighter, more like!"

"Well, whatever Diego, your music is something else."

Nessie offered him a cigarette and retrieving it, he replied, "Maybe."

Nessie lit his cigarette and said, "Looks like I'm ahead again."

Diego smiled and took a thoughtful drag on his cigarette. "You can tell me it's none of my business, but I can't imagine Michael took it very well when you told him he'd have to wait some extra days for you?"

Nessie ran a hand through her hair. "It's okay, Diego, seeing as we seem to be getting dangerous again."

Diego curled his eyebrows. "We are?"

Nessie chinked Diego's whisky glass. "This is rock 'n' roll, isn't it? Drinking whisky on the Camino with a rock legend."

Diego smiled, his eyebrows dropped. "Guess so."

They took a sip of whisky and Nessie said, "Seriously though, I had to pluck up the courage to do it. After I left you I arrived here and spent most of the next day mooching around and pondering it over. Finally, this morning, I did it. Messaged him to say that this is my walk and I'm not altering it for anyone. When I arrive in Tui he can walk alongside me if he likes, but I'm not going to do things just to suit him. We'll have to stay in *albergues* on separate bunks, and if he can't keep up with me, tough."

Diego blew some smoke through his nose and grinned. "Guess he couldn't say much to that."

Her irritated-looking expression brightened. "Nope, this little dragon is furious!" This time it was Diego's turn to chink Nessie's glass.

They found themselves talking about their childhoods and where they had grown up. Learning they were both from country towns. Reflecting on the people and events that still made them laugh when they thought about them.

Nessie's eyes were already watering as she recalled one funny story. "There had been this overweight man whom everyone in the town knew, but not just because he was so fat. You see, he was incredibly precious about his large car – a BMW I think it was. It was immaculate, and apparently he polished it every day. Anyways, one day someone in another car parked bumper to bumper against his. It was outside the local pub on the high street. The podgy man had only just parked his car and he was furious. He was effing and blinding. He was so loud he drew everyone out of the pub and the surrounding shops to see what all the fuss was about. I had been in the pub with my parents. That was funny enough, but when he got out of his BMW and approached the man from the other car, you'll never guess. His trousers fell down."

Nessie grabbed Diego's arm and leaned into him as she convulsed with laughter. After a moment she caught her breath. "He was wearing the largest Y-front underpants I think anyone had ever seen on a man."

"That's funny," said Diego smiling and glancing down at Nessie's hand on his arm.

Noticing Diego's observation, Nessie removed her hand. "I still remember the look of both surprise and shame across his face. It's that look that still cracks me up. Better than Benny Hill."

"Benny Hill?"

"It was one of the classic comedy shows on television from back in the day. They used to show repeats on TV and I loved it."

"Well, sounds like you couldn't make that story up," said Diego, offering Nessie his handkerchief.

Nessie shook her head and wiped her laughter tears away. When she had finally regained her composure they talked more about their small-town memories. Wondering if a life like that was ever possible to experience again. Nessie had grown up near Swansea, and after studying chemistry at Bristol University, had continued to live in Bristol as she'd managed to secure a good job there with a pharmaceutical company. Naturally, Michael had followed her to the city too.

Later, when the shadows from the buildings were lengthening across the river, Dave grabbed the attention of a waiter and asked him if there was anywhere to go dancing in the town. They learned that there was a popular beach nightclub. Grinning, Dave turned to the Koreans and Nessie and asked, "*Señoras* would you like to come dancing tonight?" The Koreans glanced briefly at each other, and then smiled, nodding their heads in unison.

"Why not, it'll be fun," said Nessie. She glanced at Diego. "You're up for it too?"

Diego drew deeply on his cigarette. He felt the road on his feet and the excesses of his drinking swirling around his body, but meeting Nessie again was a stroke of luck, a gift.

He'd find some reserves from somewhere. He stubbed his cigarette into an ashtray, smiled and said, "Sounds like a great idea, but first I need to find a hotel."

The Spaniard and Englishman arranged to meet the girls later that night at the club. Nessie showed the Koreans the town's pilgrim *albergue*, which she'd stayed at the night before, and they all checked in. The men found a simple but clean hotel along a narrow street, beside a chapel with a spherical Moorish-style dome. Dave insisted on having his own room, which suited Diego fine.

It felt as if Diego had hardly popped his sleeping pills when he was awoken by a knock on the door and Dave shouting his name. Diego's eyes blinked open but he preferred to wrap himself back up in the dream he'd been having about Mari. Her lengthy fringe had been streaked with silver hairs, and he'd sensed her curiosity. Diego scrunched his eyes, trying to recapture more of the dream, however, all he glimpsed was the hem of Mari's flamenco dress, swirling as she turned down a forest path, autumn leaves falling behind her. The knocking continued and Mari's image was completely lost. Diego flinched and jumped out of the bed. He opened the door.

Dave's headphones were hugging his neck and emitting their ubiquitous salsa rhythms. Grinning and moving his shoulders to the music he asked. "Did you sleep? Found it impossible myself."

"Actually, I was. What time is it?"

"Time to let the dogs out!"

"*¿Qué?*"

"Never mind," replied Dave as he reached into his pocket for his phone and checked the time. "Just after seven."

Diego leaned into the doorframe. "It's a bit early, isn't it?"

"Come on, thought we could check out the scene before we hook up with the chicks."

Diego sighed. "Give me a few minutes to take a shower and I'll meet you downstairs."

"Wicked!"

Diego closed the door and went into the bathroom. Peeling off his shirt and jeans, he shivered. His head felt cloudy. Nevertheless, he felt certain the shower and a few drinks would sort out his hangover.

THEY STROLLED through the town and arriving at the beach they came to the nightclub, which was in a renovated fort. Dave casually walked through its main gate, followed by Diego. It was near empty. Staff were preparing the bar for the night and a young couple were sitting at a corner table. Diego bought himself a beer and Dave had a Coke. They ascended stone steps to the ramparts, found themselves a table and angled their chairs to face the sea.

"What d'you reckon Diego, this is the life," commented Dave as he pulled out from under his shirt a small bottle of vodka and proceeded to pour a measure into his glass.

Diego laughed. "No wonder your vacation is so cheap, *amigo.*"

"You won't get me paying club prices," Dave replied, hiding the bottle under their table.

"Fair enough, but I would have bought you a drink."

"Mate, you may be a rock star but I can pay my way."

Diego raised his beer bottle. "I'll drink to that."

As they drank, they observed the seabirds hovering above the shoreline before they flapped in the direction of their night's sanctuary. Diego tilted his head up at the first stars, observing, "No artificial lighting needed here above the dance floor. Especially with that low star."

"That's not a star – it's Jupiter," Dave said casually.

"It is. How do you know that?"

"Read it."

"You like reading, right?"

"Prefer to find out things for myself. Don't trust the bull-shit that most people spout." Dave took a sip from his glass. "So, how did you become a rock star – can't say I know your music to be honest."

Diego turned his gaze away from Jupiter and took a thoughtful sip of beer before he murmured, "Hmm, *former* rock star."

"You don't sound too convinced?"

"What is it they call it? That's it... I think I'm having an identity crisis."

"I stopped trying to figure out who I'm meant to be a long time ago, makes life simpler."

"Perhaps that's the best way?"

Dave glanced up at the sky. "All them stars up there are made of fragments of dust and gasses that collided millions of years ago. And us, mate, here, we're just a random bit of this and that, too. So I figure it's better just to get on with it and enjoy the moment."

Diego took another sip of beer, composing his response. "So, *amigo*, you don't think there's any benefit in making plans, or committing to people?"

"Depends who's making the plans," offered Dave. He nodded back up at the stars. "Only knowledge in the universe is God's, or whatever you want to call Him. Not some geezer's interpretation of it."

"What do you mean?"

"Man's interpretation of everything."

Dave's answer brought to mind the inscription on the stone Diego had read with Nessie: '*A pen creates but also destroys nature,*' and now, it began to make some sense. Diego raised his chin and said, "You're certainly a thinker, Dave."

"Don't think too many people would agree with you on

that one, mate," replied Dave, raising his glass. "But I'll take it, nonetheless."

Diego raised his glass and they chinked them together, saying, "*¡Salud!*" in unison and Dave added, "*¡Olé!*"

They drank and Diego found himself asking, "But seriously, as a kid, you never had a burning ambition to be something?" He grinned. "Perhaps an astronaut?"

Dave got up and said, "Nah, just a gigolo," as he glanced over the railings. "Another drink?"

"Yes, but…"

They were disturbed by the arrival of the girls and Dave wrapped his arms around the Koreans. "Alright girls, what's your tipple?"

The Koreans smiled gleefully as they acknowledged the term, and both requested beers. Nessie ordered a beer too. Diego pushed out three chairs, gesturing the girls to sit down. When Dave arrived back with the drinks they paired off again. Spotlights were now encircling the club's stone walls, and the place was getting busier. The beats of electronic dance music were pulling up people to the dance floor and Dave led Ha-eun and Aera down the steps to dance, leaving Diego and Nessie alone. "Whisky?" suggested Diego, noticing a passing waitress and Nessie agreed with a grin. He ordered a bottle with ice and a Coke mixer for Nessie.

The whisky soon arrived and Diego poured Nessie a glass from the bottle. "Ice?" he asked.

"Please, and a good measure of Coke."

Diego added some Coke and ice to her drink and said, "Is that your favourite tipple when you're out on the town in Swansea or Bristol?"

"Good word, tipple, don't you think? Makes you think of tipsy and drunk." Diego nodded a little pensively and Nessie continued. "But yes, that's what I like to drink in a club or somewhere like that."

Diego poured himself a large measure of whisky and took

a long drink. He felt irritable and agitated. Thinking about it for a moment, he realised it was the same mood that had often consumed him after another one of his long drinking sessions. He usually drank at length when he'd had some free time in between his music commitments. Diego supposed he hadn't been pleasant to be around during those times. He wanted to be in Nessie's company, yet he didn't know how to shake off his present fog. Worse, the place reminded him of his wedding party. They had been married in a mock castle hotel, beside an Andalucían beach. An image of himself and Mari flashed across his mind. Mari bunching up the hem of her long wedding dress as they danced the night away amongst their guests.

Finally, Nessie said, "Diego. Is something wrong?"

He winced, and put his whisky glass on the table. "*Lo siento*, I mean sorry, I'm not really into this tonight."

"That's okay. You're probably bored of clubs?"

"You could say that. Don't you find this music irritating?"

"I agree, not much substance to these songs."

Diego stood up and turned towards the balcony. Gripping it hard he looked down at the dance floor. Instantly he spotted the Korean girls with Dave. Aera was riding high on Dave's shoulders and swinging her arms above her head. Ha-eun was shaking her head as she danced, her glossy dark hair swirling around her. The floor was a bobbing mass. Diego turned his gaze back to Nessie and shouted, "Want to get out of here?"

"Yes!" she yelled back.

Diego grabbed the bottle of whisky and they dashed down the stairs and out of the club. Outside, Diego wanted to get as far away as possible from the music. So they removed their shoes and walked across the beach towards the shore-line. Arriving at the water, they turned left in the direction of the rocky outcrop of the bay.

Reaching the rocks and feeling a breeze across his face Diego said, "It'll soon be autumn."

"I like autumn," replied Nessie as she wrapped her arms around her chest. Sensing she was cold, Diego removed his jacket and hung it over her shoulders.

"You're sure? Now you'll be cold," said Nessie.

Diego shook his head firmly. "I'll be fine." He forced a smile, sweeping his arms across the rippling contours of the ocean. "After all, I'm el Relámpago – the Lightning, there's electricity running through my veins! Or at least that's what Ha-eun and Aera seem to believe."

Nessie laughed and slid her arms into the jacket and its tassels flapped in the wind. They went over to the rocks and sat down on the leeward side. Diego took a glug of whisky and handed the bottle to Nessie.

After she'd taken a drink she said, "Do you think people would say we're both on the Camino because we're running away?"

Nessie handed Diego the bottle and he took another sip as he pondered over the question. "I don't know. I'm not sure if anyone really knows what I want, or why I do things. I'm not sure I know myself."

Nessie drew in some breath to speak but paused momentarily, then said, "Hand me the bottle." Diego passed Nessie back the bottle and she gulped down some whisky. Next, she placed the bottle upright in the sand and leaning back on her elbows but still looking at him she said, "I think I am running away, but perhaps there's also a reason for it. To go on a journey and meet the person you're truly meant to be with. Could that be you, Diego?"

He quivered with anxiety. He wasn't prepared for this; Nessie's honesty had caught him off guard. It felt like a new flamenco technique to learn and react to, a *palo*, that he wasn't experienced enough to strum. Still, he felt lonely and he missed being intimate with a woman. Diego dropped back on his elbows and turned to face her. "Perhaps you're right, Nessie. Maybe that's why we've encountered each other on this Camino. To feel the emotion of life together." Diego hated that those words had rolled off his tongue as quickly worded lyrics, clichéd and without much thought, but designed to charm nonetheless. He knew it was wrong but he couldn't stop himself.

He looked into Nessie's eyes, which had brightened like a silver moon. He leaned in and kissed her neck. He felt her tremble, perhaps she was shivering, but then she relaxed. Diego then removed the jacket from her and spread it across the sand. Next, he placed his hands on her waist and kissed her lips, circling his arms around her, and they fell back onto his jacket. Diego could smell seaweed, though the aroma of Nessie's perfume softened it somewhat. They tangled themselves in one another, Nessie's long hair falling forward, dark shapes clawing against the rocks, the moonlight occasionally lighting their faces. A bat swooped above them and the sea gurgled as it pulled away from the shoreline.

After they had made love, Diego immediately reached for the whisky bottle and sprang up. Facing out to sea he drank from the bottle, only turning around after a minute or two to face Nessie. He looked down at her and offered her the bottle. But she refused it, brushing him away with a shake of her head. Diego took another swig, then uttered, "We'd better go."

They barely spoke as they wandered across the beach and through the town. Arriving at Nessie's hostel, they found a middle-aged woman locking the front door. She ushered Nessie in, stiffly reminding her of the curfews at the pilgrim *albergues*. Diego kissed Nessie on the cheek, saying he hoped to see her along the road.

"You're a worthless shit!" screamed Nessie as she stepped back and threw Diego's jacket back at him. She turned away, not wanting to look over her shoulder as she went inside. She didn't want Diego to see her eyes were now filled with tears.

Diego put his jacket on and headed towards the river. At a riverside wall, he took a seat and resumed drinking the whisky. Moored in the murky water was a replica galleon. He glared beyond it towards the dark profile of the bridge they'd earlier crossed. He felt determined to finish the bottle, not knowing how to account for himself anymore. He noticed the looming shadow outline of a convent on the hills above the town and the bridge. It was grey, austere, judgemental. Diego drank some more, thinking he was experiencing some kind of punishment. *Why did I do that?* He smoked a cigarette and greedily finished off the whisky. Then he looked up at the convent and tossed the bottle into the water. All that was left was to go to bed.

The sound of a mop plunging into a bucket and the bitter smell of bleach outside his door awoke Diego. He squinted in the wedges of sunlight coming through the slats of the window blind and closed his eyes again, hoping to fall back to sleep, but his head was thumping hard and there was no avoiding his hangover. He slowly uncoiled his body and sat up in the bed. Glancing down, he noticed his discarded shirt and sleeping pills spilling out of the plastic bottle across the floor. Diego placed his hands on the side of his head, bending his torso towards the sheets. "It's time to go back," he whispered.

Suddenly, a knock on the door and a booming voice diverted his agonising. "Alright! Wakey-wakey!"

Diego sighed, removed his hands from his head and twisted his neck towards the door. He cleared his throat and shouted back, "Dave?"

"Of course, your favourite cockney."

Diego slid painfully out of bed. He was still wearing his jeans and he stumbled over to the door and opened it. Dave rubbed his hands enthusiastically together, his backpack hanging over one shoulder. "Cracking night, eh!"

Diego left Dave standing in the doorway and sat back down on the bed. "How do you do it?" he groaned.

"Do what, mate?"

"Have so much energy? After a late night, a very late one, I assume?"

Dave smiled, "Yep, that Aera was good as gold," and his smile broadened into a grin. "Anyway, I presume you got lucky? We saw you and Nessie leave together."

"I don't want to talk about it." Diego glanced at his watch – it was just after nine.

Noticing Diego looking at his watch Dave noted, "Yep, time to get back on the road… Nice Rolex, by the way."

"I might take a day off from walking."

"Come on mate, get your shit together. I just heard there's a banging festival at a coastal town further along the Camino – and today's the last day."

Going to a festival was the last thing Diego felt like doing, but he found himself thinking. *What would Mari do?* His answer came immediately. *She'd have dusted herself off and headed straight there.* He rose from the bed and said, "Meet me outside in ten. Actually, better make it twenty."

ALONG THE BOARDWALKS

Diego descended the stairs of the hotel. Arriving at its small reception, he placed his pack beside the guest computer and pulled out the chair. He breathed heavily and prepared himself for Mark's response, hoping for confirmation that he was now untethered from his old world. He logged onto his account and at the top of his growing inbox was an email from Gracia.

Naturally, she was concerned about Diego and enquired about his whereabouts, but in her professional manner, she briefed him with the key information he needed to know. Gracia had returned to Madrid and dropped off his luggage at his penthouse. Diego figured she would have made the link between his irrational behaviour and Mari's disappearance. After all, she would have noticed her missing clothes when she'd hung his in the wardrobe. Yet, she didn't ask about Mari – she was too thoughtful to do that.

Diego sighed and leaned back into the chair, wrapping his hands behind his head as he briefly contemplated the sense of continuing to walk. Returning to the email, Gracia also mentioned she had met up with Mark, and that he was very keen for Diego to sign some documents, most notably one regarding the switchover of his royalties. After that, all their ties would be relinquished, including his commitments with the record company. *I love Gracia,* he thought. *But he's a snake.* He realised Mark would want to get a contract in his hands as soon as possible before he might get a grip on his emotions and change his mind.

He knew signing such a contract would be *loco,* though in that same moment, he recalled that Camarón de la Isla, the famous *cantaor,* flamenco singer, had maintained that he was not interested in money (though he appeared to have had a lot of it). The singer had also claimed that others had made far more at his expense. Diego consoled himself by thinking that perhaps that was just the way of the artist.

Just as soon as he knew of a hotel to send the contract to, he'd let her know, he said to Gracia in his reply. He also apologised, concluding his email by saying she might want to call his accountant. Only to check that everything was being paid, as normal. After he'd sent the message, his eyes scanned the other emails. To his surprise, there was one from Mari. It read:

I saw the news that the tour has been cancelled! Are you okay? Have you thought it over enough? But as you're making big decisions, it only felt right to let you know that I'm currently in San Sebastian. It feels strange, being here on my own. But it's also beautiful sitting on the hotel balcony, just thinking and enjoying the views of the sea and watching the birds swooping around.

I also wanted to say I'm sorry about the way I left. But if it makes you feel any better, this isn't easy for me and I didn't make my decision lightly.

Diego's immediate thought was to travel up to San Sebastian to catch Mari. Though, just as instinctively, he knew it wouldn't be the right thing to do. He got up and went over to the window and through it saw Dave pacing up and down the street. Diego glanced back at the computer. Returning to it, he transcribed his reply in his mind. He sat back down and typed:

Mari

What a surprise you're in San Sebastian.

I don't blame you for taking off. I was too caught up in my career; I see that now. So, truly, I'm sorry for my behaviour. But, I also want to say thank you, as you've forced me to confront what I'm doing with my music and my life. That's why I've cancelled the tour. What I'm going to say next will sound crazy, but I've decided to walk another Camino – the Camino Portugués, to give myself some space too. I'm currently in a town not far from Porto. Funny to think you're on the north coast of Spain, which is the direction this Camino takes me.

Love, Diego

Mari was also online, and almost instantly she replied:

I had been thinking we should meet at some point to talk, once we'd both had some breathing space. I thought that might have been after your tour in a couple of months. But, strangely, you're now heading north – perhaps our paths are destined to be intertwined? I was planning on spending a couple more weeks up here and avoiding the heat of Madrid. So timing-wise it would work out if I came to

*Santiago and meet you after your walk. What do you
think?*
  Ciao, Mari x

Diego's dark eyes lightened with astonished happiness,
though almost immediately he squeezed them shut as he
thought, *Man, what if she discovered that I slept with the first
backpacker I met? What if I caught something from Nessie!* He
reopened his eyes, loathing himself for just thinking that. He
recognised his time with Nessie had been special. But it was
too late to think that; he knew he had ruined things with her.
"*¡Qué Cabrón!*" he muttered. "I'm no better than Dave."
Thinking about things for a moment, he realised he still had
the walk. The Camino was the only road he'd ever been
happy on. Was this not his exit ramp from all the mistakes
he'd made in the past? Was it affording him a second chance
with Mari? Wasn't it a sign that they were now converging on
the same coast? He quickly tapped out a reply:

---

*Mari, I'm so happy. I would love to see you in
Santiago. It would be a great place to talk, and to
make plans that work for us both. Maybe we could
travel together afterwards? I will keep you posted on
my progress via email.*
  See you soon.
  Love, Diego

He sprang up from the computer and eagerly pulled his
pack over his shoulders. Stepping out of the hotel, he could
feel his feet swelling in his boots, but he couldn't give a damn
about the appropriateness of his walking footwear. He
adjusted his broad-brimmed hat and dismissed Dave's exas-

perated expression by striding ahead. As he walked, Diego also remembered he missed smoking real tobacco and resolved to dump his cigarettes later, in favour of some tobacco and roll-up papers.

The Camino waymarks led them along backstreets to a small town where they had a breakfast of coffee and croissants. They sat outside a working men's club with a café-cum-bar. Mounted on its concrete façade were fading brass plaques of various associations. Opposite was a church with a rusty bell. Dave reported he'd escorted Aera back to her hostel as the sun was coming up. He also mentioned he'd seen Nessie leaving the hostel at the time but that she hadn't hung around to talk. Hearing that, Diego knew it was unlikely he'd ever see her again, picturing that she'd already put some distance between themselves on the trail. He was partly relieved, but he also felt a sense of emptiness and loss.

The path resumed along the coastline, and with his hangover beginning to recede and not wanting to dwell any longer on Nessie or think too much about himself, he resolved to learn more about the man walking alongside him. So when they stopped for a smoke at a point where the Camino directed them to the boardwalks, between puffs Diego asked, "Dave, what's your surname?"

Dave observed a large wave crashing onto the shingle and quipped, "Smith."

"Hmm, *amigo*. Didn't see you as Smith – isn't it quite a common British name?"

"Does it matter what my surname is?" snapped Dave. "A rose by any other name would smell just as sweet."

Unshaken by Dave's reaction, Diego took another drag on his cigarette as he watched an old man raking dried seaweed into haystack shapes on the beach. He tilted his head in the man's direction and replied, "You believe he'd have a problem disclosing his surname to anyone?"

Dave replied with an irritable two-beat laugh. "I'd say he doesn't get asked that question very often."

"What makes you say that?"

"'Cause he's probably lived his entire life here. Everyone knows who he is, and most likely he's got children and grandchildren all with his name, too."

Diego noticed the shadow of his torso and Stetson stretching across the sand and asked, "You ever thought about having kids?"

Dave's willowy shadow shuddered across the sand. "Parents have got to care," he offered bluntly, before flicking the butt of his cigarette into the sand and continuing walking.

Diego took a final puff of his cigarette, noticing the railings of the boardwalk casting a parallel line across the wooden slats and disappearing at a point where the walkway rounded the slope of a dune. He didn't understand Dave's reaction, nor for that matter his own mind much, though there was no denying their current direction. He removed his leather jacket and stuffed it in his pack, then drank a slug of his remaining water and set off after Dave.

The boardwalks weaved a path through the dunes and long stretches of beach. Dave kept up a brisk pace and Diego was happy to trail behind him. They came across fellow walkers but soon passed them as neither pilgrim were much in the mood for conversation. Dave was plugged into his music, and Diego was trying to draw meaning from his new environment. They passed an old windmill; more seaweed harvesters; and concrete and glass houses with sea views. At one point the path twisted around a golf course with lush fairways and zipping golf carts. Diego wondered how long it might be before the old ways were completely lost to progress.

Eventually the boardwalk veered right, ending at a dusty track beside a windswept cork tree, and they soon passed through a couple of cobbled hamlets, landmarked by churches. Arriving in Fão, they purchased a baguette from a bakery and cheese and colas from a minimarket. They made sandwiches and had lunch in the shade of a cemetery wall. Next, the route took them to an estuary with an expansive steel bridge. Diego spied a café and insisted they catch their breath before the final push into Esposende and the festival. Coffee won, and they sat on a bench by the waterside watching moored fishing vessels turning in the currents of the blue water.

"I like you Dave, but I don't get you at all," said Diego after a while.

"You barely know me," replied Dave, his attention turning to the bright backpacks of two ladies moving across the bridge.

"That's the point, mate! You won't give me a chance to get to know you better."

Dave took a sip of his coffee and then replied, "My childhood was crap and I've been in prison. I'm not forcing you to hang around if you find that worrying."

Diego laughed loudly. "You're probably the most interesting person I've met in years. Why would I suddenly want to push off?" He controlled his laughter and offered Dave a cigarette. "Man, you think I walk on water or something?"

Dave accepted the cigarette and said, "It doesn't matter what I think. You're famous, and in the eyes of the world, you're banging."

"Maybe… But so are you from where I'm sitting."

"What!?" Dave felt his eye twitching; he covered the side of his face with a hand and turned his attention back to the estuary.

"You're brave, for starters."

"You think so?" Strangely, Dave felt he could trust Diego. He dropped his hand from his face and discovered himself saying, "Well, is it so brave of me to go by a false name. You know, my name isn't really Dave."

"Well, I shouldn't be surprised given your surname isn't Smith." Diego lit their cigarettes "So, who am I smoking with?"

After a long drag on his cigarette and watching its smoke threading towards the water, he responded, "My name is Daniel Rodgers, but you can call me Flash, if you like? That's what they used to call me back in the Bush, at the salsa club."

"Flash?"

"Yeah, after Flashdance, on account of my smooth salsa moves."

Diego winked. "Not after Flash Gordon, then?"

Daniel grinned. "I never saw it that way… A superhero, nice! "But, I think I prefer Dan if that's okay?"

Diego reached out a hand towards him. "*Mucho gusto* Dan, my name is Diego García Augusto."

Dan shook Diego's hand. "That's quite a mouthful!"

"We also take our mother's surname in Spain; hers was Augusto."

"Was?"

"*Sí*," said Diego softly. He took a drag on his cigarette, then added, "Must remember to buy some tobacco. I prefer roll-ups." He fidgeted, adjusted his hat and continued, "My mother died when I was a young kid and my papá is no longer with us."

"Life can be torture. Never really knew my parents…"

"…Are you adopted?"

"Nah – though I experienced a lot of foster parents."

"But Rodgers is the family name of your real parents?"

"Suppose so?"

"But why lie about your first name?"

Dan stared again at the bridge, stretching his view to where it touched the opposite riverbank. Then he began talking.

The only parental memory he had was standing in the doorway of a room and seeing a tall man in a uniform bending over a cot. But after briefly looking at the baby, the figure began shouting at a cowering blonde lady next to him, presumably his mother. He and his sister, Becky, had been moved around numerous foster homes for the majority of their childhoods. Dan blamed himself for all the changes, admitting he was a handful and never much took to being told what to do by people he considered strangers. Becky, on the other hand, settled in more easily with each new family. However, she was a loyal sister and would refuse to leave his side every time he had caused a problem with their foster parents and were pushed on to other foster homes. Not long after turning sixteen, everything seemed to change for the better for Dan, though. He made a couple of friends at his latest school and was taking an interest in some of his classes. With his behaviour improving, their current foster parents decided to apply for legal adoption of them both.

During this time Dan's history professor, Lyn, an attractive woman he described as having long flowing hair and wearing "classy" dresses, became aware of his potential and began giving him extra tuition. Additionally, his chemistry professor, a slim, athletic man, was also encouraging Dan in his classes. Dan would go to Lyn's flat for the extra lessons, and one evening after studying, she'd offered him a glass of wine. She'd passed it to him casually and with a gentle smile. They chatted about London, life, and for the first time, he'd felt almost equal with an adult. His desire for her came quickly. Then during another evening at her flat, he confessed to Lyn that he loved her. Lyn was shocked and immediately ended the extra studying. She also tried to avoid his eye in class, but that only encouraged Dan to try harder to regain her attention. To make things worse, one day he had spotted his chemistry professor and Lyn getting into her car. Straightaway he suspected they were having an affair.

Dan began spying on Lyn, and during one lunch break, he again saw her and his chemistry professor together, approaching her car. This was like a red rag to a bull. Dan had jumped on his cycle, chasing Lyn's car through the busy traffic of Shepherd's Bush. He followed them to a pub car park on the banks of the River Thames and witnessed them kissing inside the car. It felt like a betrayal. The next sequence of events was something of a blur, although he did remember standing outside Lyn's flat the same night and unloading gasoline across her car. The fuse to set the car on fire was the cigarette he was smoking. It took only a few hours for the police to arrive at Dan's foster home. He spent the next two years in a juvenile prison.

Gazing across the water, Dan remarked, "Reality is, most people don't give a shit what your name is. Whether it's in school, prison or the workplace."

Diego stood up and tipped the remains of his coffee into the river. "I don't think you believe that..."

"I don't?"

"What about the foster parents who wanted to adopt you? And you wouldn't be walking to Santiago if you didn't believe you counted. Deep down, you believe there is a place in this world for you, too. Not for Dave, or whoever else you've gone by in the past, but for Dan... for Daniel." The wind picked up and feeling the ocean breeze across his cheeks, Diego said enthusiastically, "My hangover has finally gone! Come on, let's get ourselves to that festival."

Dan reached for his pack and sprang up. Grinning, he said, "I noticed a couple of cute chicks crossing the bridge earlier... perhaps we'll get their names at the festival?"

"Perhaps we will, Dan."

THE COCKNEY REBEL

Bunting hung high in the streets as they wandered into the busy plaza full of stalls for the festival; the air was curdled with the hot greasy aromas of sugar and meat. Diego and Dan sat themselves down at the terrace of a bar, ordered bottles of beer and were still there when the moon emerged.

"Another?" asked Diego.

Dan glanced at their small collection of empty bottles and shaking his head replied, "Nah mate, let's grab something to eat from one of the stalls and see if we can find out where all the action is – must be a stage and music somewhere?"

"Sure," Diego answered, although after eating, he'd have preferred to return to their table to watch the comings and goings of the plaza. He'd discovered himself observing a middle-aged man serving a long line of children at his churros stand and had been admiring some of the craft stalls from afar, reminiscing about his time busking in Granada and selling Nadav's art.

"Come on, mate!" urged Dan. "What you waiting for?"

They collected their packs and went to a stall selling pork sandwiches, which they paired with cold cans of beer. The stall owner's wife mentioned a plaza where they'd find music, and they ate their sandwiches on the way. As they walked, Diego noticed symbols of the town's fishing tradition everywhere; statues dedicated to fishermen and papier-mâché fish hanging from streetlamps. They arrived at the plaza, which was boxed in by tall buildings, although it was the heart of the old town. It was also crowded, with people gathering around a music stage, waiting for the concert to begin. Diego didn't fancy jostling his way through the crowd and felt conscious about being recognised, so he made an excuse to buy some more beer. However, he was also curious to take a closer look at a tiny chapel they had just passed.

He doubled back into the cobbled thoroughfare, stopped beside the chapel and placed his face against its bottle-green window. It was small, an alcove in the façade of an apartment block, hosting an image of the cross and artificial candles. Abruptly, in the reflection of the glass, at his shoulder level, he glimpsed an elderly man with dark eyes beneath the brim of his crumpled baseball cap. Diego felt the chill of the ocean in his bones and he wound up saying, "¿Papá?"

"*Perdão?*" responded the man in Portuguese.

Diego stepped aside and although the man displayed the wrinkles of working life, he was slimmer than his father had been and was wearing a hoodie, which Papá would never have worn. Sheepishly Diego said in Spanish, "*Lo siento*, not sure why I said that?"

"Don't worry about it." The old man's voice was gravelly. As he unlocked the chapel and pushed the stiff door open, he whispered, "Your father, he has passed?"

"How did you guess that?"

"Perhaps you were considering lighting a candle for him?"

The man was right, Diego reflected. *That's why I was drawn to this little chapel.*

"*Sí*, I was." He added, "And one for my mamá too," realising he couldn't remember the last time he'd paid his respects to his deceased parents.

"Well come on in," said the man beckoning Diego through the door, "I was just coming to collect today's takings, but every extra counts."

Diego raised a smile and followed the man into the dimly lit space and asked, "You're the caretaker?"

The man responded to Diego's question with a subtle nod. Diego rested his pack in a corner, before taking a step towards the candles and placing a couple of Euro coins in the slot. In the light of the candles, he noticed, lining the lower length of the walls, the enduring *azulejo* tiles with their pale blue floral designs. Diego went over to the cross – it was protected inside a glass cabinet, lit by lights, and a carving of Jesus was mounted on it.

He removed his hat, bent his head and said a prayer for his parents. The old man emptied the coin tray from underneath the candles, and the sounds of the jangling coins seemed to bring some comfort to Diego. He recalled the numerous bridges he'd already crossed on his way, his feet trusting their steel frames to carry him safely above the waterways. He reminded himself that whatever happened with Mari, he wasn't going back to his old life. Step by step and bridge by bridge, his old path would connect to the new one.

Diego turned around to see the old man leaning against the door and gesturing with open palms. He asked, "Are you okay, son?"

Stepping towards him, Diego noticed the man had a couple of missing fingers and the lines across his pink palms ran deep and dark. "I'm fine, *gracias*. Were you a fisherman?"

"It's mostly fishermen you'll find passing by here."

"Why's that?"

The man nodded at the cross and said, "To pay their respects to the Lord of the Hills."

"You mean Jesus?"

"Yes, Christ, the Divine. Before this chapel, the sculpture was just a simple painted stone cross, mounted on the hills above the town. Fishermen would use it as a landmark to navigate. But they also knew it was protecting them from the dangerous afflictions of the sea."

"According to tradition."

"You doubt this?"

"No, not necessarily, you got to trust in something... I guess?" Diego paused, then whispered, "Just like the bridges."

"Well, the fishermen never lost their faith in the cross; even when it lost its usefulness as a maritime landmark with the town modernising and growing into the hills. They understood the cross' greater place and they transferred it here, constructing this chapel to protect it. Come dawn, I'll be opening the doors again for the fishermen so they can pray before they take their boats out and confront the ocean for another day."

Diego glanced down at the dark flagstones underfoot, as if he was trying to recall a distant thought. Then he remembered the word he was looking for, and tilting his head back up he said, "*¡Inori!*"

"That's a fancy word, son."

"It's something I think I've lost touch with. Hmm, not sure I can rightly explain its significance immediately. But meeting you and another fisherman, just recently, has reminded me of the word. The other man, he's also retired from fishing, but he's far from being done with life."

The man glanced through the window in the direction of the sea. "If fishing taught me anything, it's that life is too short. Not one for sitting at home and looking at old photos and trying to recall the good old days, or thinking if only I'd had a little more time, or I was younger. This job gets me up early, and sometimes I take tourists around the harbour."

"Can I buy you a beer?" Diego found himself asking.

The furrows across the man's forehead curled like ripples in the ocean and he smiled gently. "That's a nice offer, but I still recognise I'm an old man and I need my sleep."

"Fair enough," said Diego, reaching for his pack, and he left the chapel with the man.

They shook hands and in the man's coarse palm Diego again felt the presence of his papá. He departed and Diego watched him ambling steadily along the thoroughfare before he merged with the other strollers. The path connected both ends of the old town but it also formed part of the Camino. Diego hovered in the slant of light coming through the window and the candles and contemplated *Inori* further. Thinking that both of those old fishermen he'd met had no regrets; new endeavours and enthusiasm ensured their rivers didn't run dry. The candles went out and Diego turned towards the rock anthem sounds coming from the plaza. The shadows of the townsfolk moved softly across the old walls, and momentarily, Diego thought upon the idea that carrying a guitar by his side wouldn't feel too burdensome.

Arriving at the plaza he saw Dan standing in its far corner. He skirted his way around the crowd towards him.

"Aye aye *amigo*!" cried Dan noticing him approaching.

"How's it going?"

"The *chicas* aren't biting." Dan stood back slightly, observing Diego fully. "Did you buy any beers?"

"Er, no. I forgot."

"No worries. I've just learned of somewhere we can get a drink and definitely be in the company of ladies."

Diego stared at Dan quizzically. "A strip club?"

"Sort of."

Diego paused to think. "Ah, that kind of place!"

"Chill, *hombre*. No one's forcing you to come with me."

"Aren't you tired? We need to find a hotel."

Dan winked. "Perhaps they'll have rooms there."

"You're *loco*!" responded Diego, referencing a mad look in

his eyes. Dan's pupils were as dark as oil and widening across his pale eyes. Diego took a deep breath and glanced across the plaza, considering all the reasons why he shouldn't go with Dan, but he convinced himself it would be better that he stayed with his walking companion. So he replied, "Okay, let's check it out – someone's got to keep an eye on you." If he were being truthful, however, he would have recognised that he was going to the brothel for his own sake too. Hoping it might fix the empty feeling still lurking inside him.

Dan's eyes flickered excitedly. "Game on!"

"Just one drink, then that's me done for the night."

Dan grinned, lifted his pack and looped his arms through the straps. "It'll be sick; I'll buy some vodka on the way."

Dan strode through the town, occasionally stopping to ask directions from those who appeared likely abetters in his quest. After a while, they arrived in a narrow street of tenements with nondescript doors and no signage. However, at the far end, Dan caught sight of the figure of a man. He was ascending the steps from the basement of one of the houses. Before he knew it, Diego was following Dan down the same steps.

A couple of knocks on a metal door and they were inside and following a burly doorman through a velvet curtain. Candles and soft lighting lit the sparse room with scratches crisscrossing its wooden floor. The doorman led them to a bank of raised booths with synthetically upholstered banquettes. They appeared to be the only patrons. An equally large barman was drying glasses at the bar and talking with a woman with lustrous black hair. Sitting at a table to one side of the bar were a group of girls in night robes. Like cats, their eyes followed Diego and Dan to their booth.

The woman left the bar and arriving at their booth, lit their candle. She wore a blue backless dress exposing her golden brown skin. She nodded towards the girls. "You want to buy the ladies a drink?"

"Maybe," replied Dan.

"…No, just a drink for me and my friend, for now," inter-jected Diego. "You have a drinks menu?"

"No *carte*, what do you want?"

Dan leaned across the table to Diego and whispered, "Mate, I forgot the vodka on the way."

Diego glanced around the place; already he was beginning to think he'd made a mistake. "This isn't the kind of place you want to get caught sneaking in booze. Just order what you want – I'll cover it."

Their drinks soon arrived and Diego sipped tentatively on his beer. He glanced at Dan casually drinking his vodka and orange and said, "Man, this place is grim. Let's get out of here after these drinks."

"What do you mean, Diego? Don't you think the *chicas* are cute?" Dan winked towards the table of prostitutes.

"Hey, don't encourage them. You realise their drinks – or anything else – won't come cheap?"

"Chill, Diego. This is just some random town in Portugal, it's not Madrid nor London; we should fill our boots."

Moments later, two of the girls arrived at their table. They had removed their robes, revealing silky underwear and dark stockings. The slimmer and shorter of the girls, a blonde, bent down and kissed Diego on the cheek. Her lips were cold and her breath smelled of bubble gum. Yet Diego discovered himself patting the seat beside him and inviting her to sit down. Dan gestured to his girl, a brunette, to join him too. The blonde prostitute squeezed into the booth beside Diego. Already the brunette had one arm around Dan and her other under the table targeting his lower region. The hostess reap-peared with a tray containing a bottle of port and four crystal glasses. "The ladies, they like port," she asserted, filling the glasses with the dark wine.

Dan took a sip of his port and winked at Diego. "What do you think, your little one's cute?"

Diego half-heartedly raised his glass at Dan. The blonde made a suggestive comment in Diego's ear and he knew there was no point wrestling with his conscience anymore. He should just get drunk. *Screw the consequences*, he thought. *I'm still a rock star!*

Diego stood up. "Let's drink something decent." Diego turned to face the bar and gesturing to the hostess ordered a bottle of champagne. He also insisted the hostess bring the bill with the champagne. She returned and winced as the icy neck of the bottle tilted into her cleavage as she held it up to show Diego. "It's okay?" she asked.

Diego twisted his head towards her cleavage and appraised the bottle. Its label read: *Prosecco*. He was no champagne expert but his celebrity associates were fond of ordering the famous French brands. Instantly, he knew she was trying to con him with Italian sparkling wine. "Let me see the bill?" he said.

She handed it to Diego and returned to the bar to retrieve champagne flutes; whilst she was away Diego scrutinised the handwritten bill. It was almost illegible, but the total remained clear to his eye. The host returned to the table, put the slim glasses down and reached for the bottle.

Diego waved the bill in her face saying, "!¿Una broma, no?!"

"It is no joke *senhor*," replied the hostess coolly. "You pay for quality drinks and the extraordinary service we provide."

Out of the corner of his eye, Diego noticed the curtain flapping and the doorman pushing it to one side, and at the same time, the barman stepped around the bar counter. It looked as if he was gripping something behind his back, perhaps a small baseball bat. Diego felt his shoulders stiffening into his fatigued body, and he squinted across at Dan, whose eyes held the brunette's. Diego leaned across the table and whispered, "They want to charge us a thousand euros for the drinks. God knows what they'd charge for any extra services."

Dan sat up straight and suddenly became aware of both the barman and the doorman standing tall behind the hostess. Their stances were wide and they were breathing heavily. Although the barman didn't appear to be holding anything now, Diego surmised whatever he might have seen wouldn't be too far away.

"Understand?" hissed Diego.

Dan's eye began to twitch. "What's your plan?"

Diego could pay. But he didn't like to be swindled. Then again, a battering wouldn't be good for their walk either. He sighed, and said inwardly, *¡Madre mia!* The hostess folded her arms and dropped her jaw, producing an exaggerated yawn. Though in her antagonistic expression, Diego saw a glimmer of a plan. He smiled at her and palming his hands together announced, "Well at these prices, I think everyone should enjoy the drinks." He nodded at the men and said, "Please join us." Then he met the hostess's sharp eyes, before glancing towards the three remaining girls on the far table. "Everyone."

The hostess eyed Diego quizzically.

"Come on," urged Diego. "I'm inviting everyone to be the guest of a rock star."

"You're famous?"

"He is," interjected Dan. He was baffled by the plan but suddenly felt secure in Diego's new-found self-assurance. He retrieved his phone and tapped Diego's name into Google; instantly it displayed hundreds of images of Diego, all chore-ographed to project his rock star status. "Here, look," he offered, passing his phone to the hostess. She flicked through a couple of images and showed them to the men. They grouped closer around the table and curiously eyed Diego. Then they nodded at each other approvingly. The doorman turned to the hostess and whispered in her ear. She ushered the remaining girls over.

Diego stood down from the table, stepping aside to allow everyone to squeeze around it. Then he slid a hand underneath the table and dragged his backpack towards him as he sat at the end of the banquette. The hostess returned to the bar to fetch more champagne flutes, and Diego returned his hand to his pack, which was now between his legs. He stealthily pulled back the zip of its outside pocket and felt inside it for his sleeping pills. Finding the bottle, he slid them into a trouser pocket and proceeded to shake some out into his pocket.

The hostess returned with the flutes and after placing them around the table reached for the bottle. Diego jumped up and, trying to remain calm, produced a wide grin. "I'll do the honours... *por favor.*" She hesitated, and in that brief moment, Diego felt her vulnerability beneath her almost flawless façade. As she wavered, Diego softened his grin into a smile. "Please, take the weight off your feet." His smile disarmed her and she handed him the bottle. He took a step back from the table. Then he removed the foil and protective wire from around the neck of the bottle and began twisting the cork.

"This could be dangerous," he mentioned glancing at the cork, before turning towards the bar. The cork popped into his palm and he exchanged it for a handful of the pills in his pocket, before tilting the bottle at forty-five degrees and dropping them in. He placed a thumb over the top of the open bottle, hoping its fizz would soon dissolve the tablets. He turned back around and said, "*Cabelleros,*" offering the doorman and the barman the prosecco. They reached out with their glasses and Diego filled them, pausing to let the froth settle before topping them up. Next, he filled up the prostitutes' glasses. Afterwards, Dan pushed his glass out and Diego obliged him.

"Half-measures?" Dan muttered, noticing Diego hadn't waited for his glass to settle.

Diego winked. "Just making sure there's enough to go round." Then he leaned towards the hostess, but he also avoided filling her glass too high. Subsequently, he half-filled his own glass and holding it aloft gestured to everyone to raise their glasses too. "*¡A la vida!* To life," he declared.

Everyone apart from Diego proceeded to drink. Sampling his prosecco with just his tongue, he was relieved it didn't taste strange. Sitting back down, he noted the distant rumblings of thunder above the din of the synthetic music beats. Strangely, he felt the stirrings outside comforting, and he hoped his cocktail of pills would soon prove effective. He gestured with the bottle at the barman and doorman and they held out their glasses again. Diego eagerly obliged them.

Now Dan was squeezed in between the brunette and another prostitute, who caressed him as if they were one person. Diego had shuffled along from the end, and the hostess had joined him. Noting Dan enjoying the attention of the girls, she leaned into Diego and murmured, "You can have all of them, if you like?"

Diego twisted his body to face her and laughed with bemusement. "They'd ruin me!"

"You've never had more than one woman before?"

He removed his Stetson again and wafting it across his face said with a hint of irony, "One woman is enough for any man to handle."

The hostess's lips curled into a half-smile. "Hmm, you are no normal rock star."

"Perhaps? And you, you're not as cold as you make out. I noticed that smile."

She moved her lips left and right as she thought over her reply. "Only thing that separates a man from a woman is emotion, but controlling your emotions is essential in a job like this." Regaining her composure, she ran a finger across the back of Diego's hand. "Perhaps, you would like just me… for the entire night?" Diego found himself staring at her cleavage and lacy bra, but he dragged his hand away from hers and looked at his Rolex. Then he glanced up at the bouncer and barman but they were showing no signs of drowsiness. The hostess rubbed Diego's shoulder and with a wink said, "Perhaps you prefer men, no?"

Diego's eyebrows rose indignantly. His ego teased him, and he felt the urge to have her. Nonchalantly he glanced across the table towards the bar. Thinking a stiff drink would loosen any final resistance he might have for her. But as he did, his attention was caught by the blue smudge of flame, dancing within the wider blaze of the candle. Diego turned his head back to the hostess, and he asked her, "Do you feel you belong here?"

A groan from the doorman, followed by a thud, prevented her from immediately answering his question. Next, the barman yawned, and his head dipped. Then, almost immediately, his head was also resting beside the doorman's on the table. Both men were asleep and breathing heavily. Dan felt the hands of the girls loosening around his torso. They leaned back into the banquettes, and almost in unison, they fell asleep too. Moments later the remaining prostitutes were also asleep. Dan glanced across the table at Diego, his eye stuttering. The hostess shook the lumpy men and girls, but to no avail.

Diego stood up. "They're done for the night," he said turning to the hostess. "And if I were you I'd take myself home to bed too."

"What's happened?"

He showed her the sleeping pills. "Essential medicine for any rock star. Double strength you see!"

"No. You didn't?"

Diego nodded. "Very naughty, I know." He peeked at the

sleeping girls in their underwear and said, "I'd throw something over them – they'll sleep through to the morning."

Dan's face contorted into a grin. He gently leaned his girls into the wall, and then stepped around them. Diego checked his wallet for banknotes and noted he had more than a thousand euros on him. He looked up at Dan. "How much cash do you have?"

Dan fumbled around in his pockets and wallet. "Around a hundred euros."

"Okay, plenty for your share. Leave fifty on the table for the drinks."

Dan placed his fifty euros under the prosecco bottle.

Diego fingered his money attentively and then handed the bundle of notes to the hostess. "For your service."

Her head felt a little foggy. However, she cast an assertive glance at the bulky men breathing hard and slumped over the table. Then she turned and took in the full measure of the dingy space. She recalled the first time she had given her body to a punter, then vomiting after it was over and vowing she would leave. Yet here she was five years later. She clasped the money tightly and looking up at Diego said, "Thank you." Then she strolled across the bar towards a padded door leading through to the backrooms. The hostess returned a couple of minutes later wearing a belted raincoat and holding some tablecloths for blankets. In the meantime, Diego and Dan had collected their packs and the hostess paused briefly, eyeing their packs on their backs. She asked, "You are both walking this Camino?"

"We are," said Diego.

"Well, if you two can, so can I!"

The pilgrims nodded back at her, noting her sincerity. Also aware that it takes all sorts to walk the Camino.

"But first, I must sleep," the hostess added.

They all grinned conspiratorially. As they left, Diego tipped his hat at the hostess and Dan gave her the thumbs-up.

Dan leaned into Diego as his boot hit the final step leading up to the street. Diego guided Dan around a puddle and glanced up at the remaining grey clouds. Musing that it would have been good to feel the earlier rain tapping hard on his Stetson.

THE MORNING AFTER

Dan and Diego were sitting on the extensive balcony of their hotel room, wearing bathrobes and eating breakfast. "I feel like royalty," exclaimed Dan, tucking into his breakfast and admiring the uninterrupted view of the sea.

Diego acknowledged Dan by raising his coffee cup at him.

"If I had an Amex like you, I'd stay here for at least a week," said Dan.

"It's a fantastic view, but believe me, you get bored with luxury hotels after a while. They're pretty much the same wherever you stay. Same furniture, framed pictures, cooked breakfasts; same pompous guests." Diego noted their breakfast trolley dressed with a tablecloth. It was laden with porcelain, pastries, scrambled egg, sausages and fresh juice. He sipped his coffee. "Ha, I guess it's hard to give up some indulgences." He lowered his voice slightly. "But I'm sick of the bullshit; it feels good to be walking away from it all, even if I've got a little side-tracked."

Dan put his fork down. "You're not still feeling guilty? Mate, you *are*… about Nessie or last night?"

Diego stood up and glanced back into the room. "Have you seen my cigarettes?"

"Yeah, you left them in the bathroom."

"Do you want one?"

Dan shook his head, and Diego padded across the room. He returned with a cigarette in hand and placed the box and lighter on a table. Next, he leaned against the balcony railings. "Man, I had discipline when I was learning new skills with the guitar, and when I had a guitar maestro, my music professor. When I dropped all that, I developed so many bad habits. Except the one thing I never did was cheat on Mari, my wife. But, I did that the other day! And how easily I might have done it last night."

"Well, where is she now? Seems like she's given you a free pass to do whatever you want."

Diego eyeballed Dan for the audacity of his statement, but relaxed his glare almost immediately; he had already learned Dan was a plain speaker and meant well, in his own way.

Dan continued, "Have you heard of the expression 'what goes on tour stays on tour'?"

"Of course, it's a favourite expression with the music crew that I usually tour with. But why couldn't I manage to keep my *pijo* in my trousers, on this tour."

"That was then, this is now. Do you think if Mari found out about Nessie it'd influence her decision about your marriage?"

"I think she'd find it weird to know I'd been with someone else. But I'm not sure she'd care as much anymore."

Dan paused, taking a sip of his coffee as he thought. "Maybe she wants you to sleep with other people?"

Creases formed across Diego's brow as Dan's abrupt words began to cut. "*¡Qué!* What are you suggesting? So she could do the same, and feel less guilty herself?"

"I don't know, mate. But I was thinking, by sleeping with a few others, perhaps you might feel less attached to her. Maybe Mari would want you to experience that?"

"But why, then, would she have agreed to meet me in Santiago?"

Shrugging his shoulders Dan said, "Look, I'm just surmising. But from an outsider's POV, it seems she's open to your walk. Including whatever experiences or liaisons you might have on the way."

Diego lit his cigarette and turned around to face the sea, clenching the railing. He smoked his cigarette broodingly, but after a couple of minutes, he loosened his grip and turned back around to face Dan. "But what about you, Dan?"

"What do you mean?"

"It is Dan, isn't it? Or did you give me another false name?"

Dan stood up. "Wanna check my passport?"

"Sit back down," responded Diego taking his seat again. "Man, you don't have to do that." Dan returned to his chair and slouched back. "But *amigo*, seeing as we're talking openly, let me please say this. Chasing sex like you do won't make you feel any better, believe me. I was like that before I met Mari. So desperate for intimacy, but fearful of love at the same time. And before you go ahead and say it, I may be suffering because of love too… but I still believe in it."

Dan looked paler than normal and his eye was twitching. "Can I have that cigarette, please?"

Diego handed him one and they sat smoking in silence, watching a distant fishing vessel motoring out to sea. High waves battered it, yet it continued to progress, slowly. When the boat was no more than a dark spot on the horizon Dan stubbed out his cigarette and went to the bathroom. Diego lit another cigarette. Gazing at the cloudless sky and horizon, he pondered the next stage of his walk. Wondering who they might meet next.

When Dan returned from the bathroom he was showered and dressed. Diego noticed his eye was still twitching. "Mind if I bum another cigarette?" he asked Diego.

"Of course not," replied Diego, standing up. He nodded down at the balcony table where he'd left his cigarettes. "Help yourself, I'm going to take a shower."

When Diego returned from the shower he noticed Dan was pensively pacing up and down the length of the balcony. He left him to his private moment and went to get dressed. By the time Diego had dressed and gathered his things together, Dan had begun to relax, although he didn't say much. Minutes later, Dan collected his pack, and they left the room and went downstairs to check out of the hotel. Arriving outside, Diego turned right to follow the continuing trail north along the coastline. However, Dan hesitated.

Diego turned around. "What's up?"

"Mate, I feel that I might not be doing the right thing..."

"*Qué*, what do you mean?"

"I think I should be back in London."

Diego took a step back to take a better look at Dan. "What about your walk of sin?"

"I've gotta give it a go – my Colombian *chica*. Her and the kid. I can't be another person walking out on them."

"Hmm, but do you love them?"

"I'm not completely sure. But I think that's the point; I never really gave it long enough to find out. Never give anything, or anyone, much of a chance. And it's time Dora knows my real name – she still knows me as Dave, and I need to fix that."

"That could be tricky when she finds out you lied to her."

"It's a risk, I know, but you kept walking with me after I spun you the bullshit about my name."

"I did," acknowledged Diego.

"Well, what do you think, should I abandon my Camino and go back to them?"

Diego glanced towards the sea and thought of that resilient little boat he'd viewed from the balcony. Turning to face Dan again he said, "What would you do if you returned there?"

Dan blinked. "You mean for work?"

"*Sí*, for a living. I assume you burned your bridges with your job when you left for Lisbon?"

"I did, but as they say, 'London always provides', so I'll be alright."

"Hell, give it a go then. The very fact that you're even thinking this way all of a sudden shows that you must care for them. And if it doesn't work out you can always resume the Camino. Just make sure it's another Holy Year if you do!"

Daniel's face widened into a grin. "Well, I better make it work then, 'cause the next Holy Year is not for another six years."

Diego matched Dan's grin and said, "Well, that's a reason if any, to give it a go with your *chica*."

"A hundred per cent," replied Dan stretching out his hand to fist bump Diego's.

"You're returning right now?" asked Diego as he closed his fist and met Dan's gesture.

Dan signalled to one of the taxis waiting outside the hotel, and getting into the car he said, "*Gracias*, mate." No other words were needed.

Diego waved Dan off and he turned back to the sea. The day was warming up but the sea breeze was cool. He didn't need to delay signing the papers that Mark had drawn up regarding his royalties. He realised he could manage it all from here and returned to the hotel.

It didn't take long to organise things. Gracia emailed the contracts to the hotel and a receptionist printed them off for Diego to sign. Perhaps he should have had a lawyer check them over, but that had been no more than a passing thought and he didn't want to delay his walk.

He turned to leave but paused as he thought about the rest of his walk. From what Diego remembered from looking at

Nessie's guidebook, the Costa route from Porto was some twelve days or so walking, and he'd already completed at least two of them. Counting the days reminded him that it wasn't long until his and Mari's wedding anniversary; glancing at the date on his Rolex he realised it was just a week away, at the beginning of September. *It might just be possible,* he considered. Diego asked the receptionist to borrow her computer. His email to Mari stated that he had walked away from his royalties, but events had presented them with the perfect opportunity to meet in Santiago for their anniversary. Perhaps there, they could even renew their wedding vows and start afresh.

After Diego left the hotel, he crossed over to the other side of the street towards the beach. At the low sea wall, he removed his socks and boots and put them inside his pack. He rolled his jeans up his shins, stepped over the wall, and then padded across the sand to the shoreline. Arriving beside the sea, breaking waves fizzed over his feet and he smiled contentedly.

IN ANOTHER MAN'S SHOES

Diego passed the last of the boardwalks and saw a sign that directed the Camino away from the coast, pointing towards a quiet country lane. As he squeezed his feet back into his boots, he promised to buy himself some decent walking shoes as soon as he could. The Camino curled uphill towards pine trees; their tops blushed yellow by the climbing sun as they poked above the rooftops of houses built into the ridge. It wasn't long before he'd left the coastline and its urban life below, and although the sea breeze occasionally gusted into the hills, its salty grit was refined by the aroma of eucalyptus, jasmine and wild herbs.

Diego sensed Galicia in the environment and set Tui as his next target. He'd remembered from Nessie's book that, at that point, a wide river marked the border between Portugal and Spain. The idea of heading north through rural Galicia brought a smile to his face; it had been his favourite region on his first Camino, the Francés. He also noted its music remained true to its ancient roots of *música folclórica*, unlike flamenco, which some felt had strayed too far from its heritage, though, of course, he'd been complicit in that too.

After several kilometres, he arrived at a hamlet where

there was a bar with a billiard table, and he took a coffee and smoke break there. Inside he met a Bulgarian couple, who spoke some English, and were curious to know about his life. However, he didn't give much away and hid behind the language barrier. Drinking his coffee he borrowed their Camino Portugués guidebook, and spread its map section across the baize-covered table. It was written in Bulgarian, but he was able to study the map. To his disappointment he saw that this stage of the Camino path would wind back down to the coast at Viana do Castelo before the day was out. It would be at least a couple more days of boardwalks before there was an option to take a detour from the coastal path to the central Camino path, which appeared a more direct route to Santiago and should save him a day or so. There was no time to waste. Diego returned the book to the Bulgarians and quickly left, thinking there may even be an earlier way to join the Central path.

The way led along a cobblestoned street and before long, a yellow arrow spray-painted on a lamppost directed Diego past a church with nodding sunflowers in its courtyard and further uphill into a forest. Further along the path, there was a stone Camino marker, with the Knights of Santiago blood-red cross carved into the stonework. The path undulated its way through the forest, and when it dropped down to a river with a flagstone crossing, Diego stopped to catch his breath. Without thinking he reached for his hip flask and took a drink of whisky. He watched the river cascading and foaming over rocks from a higher tier upstream. He paused further, his attention drawn to the swoosh, swoosh, of the fast-flowing water.

He glanced up the ascending path ahead, which faded into a wooded canopy and a misty curtain of clouds sagging across the hillside. Diego's nostrils flared as he breathed everything in. He crossed the bridge and pushed himself hard up the steep hill.

Diego stopped for a brief lunch at a roadside café; just enough time to avoid any curious questions, eat a sandwich, drink a cold beer and smoke a cigarette. The afternoon's walking felt relentless, and he was constantly adjusting his Stetson against the sunshine that found a way through the trees. The crunch of boot over pinecone and the distant chimes of church bells provided some comfort, and he was slightly disappointed when he left the woods and arrived at the main road leading down towards a modern road bridge.

Cars jarred Diego's senses as he crossed the bridge on its pedestrian walkway, but he found some distraction in the view ahead of the marina and the elegant mansions and onion-domed church sitting on the hillside above Viana do Castelo. The sky was a rich blue, mirrored in the estuary below, which shimmered with clouds of restless juvenile fish. Arriving in the town, Diego asked a policeman where the nearest outdoor store might be, and was directed towards the heart of the town and its alleyways of shops. On the way, as he walked along the main thoroughfare, he gave a cursory glance towards rows of fake branded sports shoes and a pile of T-shirts being sold in the street by a lone African street hawker. 'USA' was embroidered on the man's baseball cap, and flecks of grey glistened around the chin of his evening stubble.

"*Amigo*," said the African ambiguously, though his follow-up remark was more emphatic when Diego met his eyes. "Your boots are very dusty. How about a pair of decent Nikes?"

Diego glanced at the rows of various pairs of Nikes spread across the man's blanket. "They look great, but they wouldn't last more than a day on a country road. Come on *amigo*, they're all fake."

The man gestured back to Diego's feet and eyeing the cowboy boots, he laughed loudly in three booming beats. "Perhaps, but I think your feet would not last long in those boots, pilgrim!" Inspecting his boots further he said, "But leather look real nice; a man might reinvent himself in those."

Diego smiled wryly. "That's probably the truth!"

The man straightened his stance and put a foot forward to display his lightweight fabric-style walking shoes. "Now these are real deal, waterproof. Brand new and perfect for walking long distance."

"*Sí*... that's exactly what I need."

"You want to trade?"

Diego focused on the walking shoes and their quality did indeed look good. Replying cautiously he said, "They're genuine, right? But we might not be the same size." He paused. "And my boots were very expensive, handcrafted in Mexico. It's not exactly an equal trade." Immediately he regretted his remark.

"I see," replied the man. "Hmm, everything has certain value at certain times. But I know about wearing good shoes for walking and travelling. Travel has been my life."

"It has?" asked Diego curiously.

The tout removed his cap; his hair was patterned snowy grey with tight spirals. He wafted the cap across his dark face as he went on to describe his itinerant life. "Migrancy", he stated, "is the plague of the 21st century. Escaping one place to seek a better life somewhere else repeatedly puts people in a worse situation. There are always new customs, rules and laws to abide by. Often, these seem strange or don't make any sense at all. And although the road has its laws, too, it is not policed in the same way and there is no freer way to live." He talked of his life travelling across the Iberian region, and the good and bad seasons for his merchandising; he described unscrupulous wholesalers, the best areas to eat tapas, and who makes the best travel companions. He also had his opinions on the best places to camp where the authorities left you alone.

He was quick to add that, although his description veered

towards the romantic, such a life was not for everyone. Modern enslavement, as he put it, is what most people seem to want. His statement momentarily put Diego in mind of how his father had chosen to live. Papá was stubborn, but even he had to make compromises so they could get by in the village. Still, his old candyfloss machine had given him much independence. Diego had played by Madrid's rules too, but he had never really settled there. He wondered if there was somewhere he and Mari would feel comfortable living.

Diego looked the man up and down and noticed his eyes were old, yet there remained vibrancy behind them. Eyes that had seen many things, and Diego discovered himself glancing back down at his walking shoes and saying, "Well man, it wouldn't do any harm to see if we have the same size feet."

A few minutes later they had swapped shoes, and both men were feeling equally satisfied with their new footwear. Diego was now able to wriggle his blistering toes more generously. He put his pack down and became more aware of the road on the rest of his clothes; he patted off the dust from his jeans and clammy shirt, then nodded at the T-shirts, noticing on the top of the stack a hoop-patterned green and white shirt. Its Lion badge revealed it was a Sporting Lisbon soccer shirt. "And I'll buy a couple of shirts from you too."

The tout passed Diego the soccer shirt as well as a T-shirt. Diego tried them against his chest for size and they seemed a good fit. He passed the man some notes from his dwindling cash and without thinking, completed the deal by offering the man a fist bump. It brought to mind Mamadou, his former Senegalese friend, who had resorted to street touting when times were tough.

Food, sleep and an early start crossed Diego's mind, and he glanced around looking for a Camino sign that might direct him to the town's municipal *albergue*. He was suddenly curious to see inside a pilgrim hostel again and embrace the pilgrim lifestyle. He couldn't spot a sign to one, but finding himself back at the bridge and the river, he noticed the lethargic paces of a couple of pilgrims exiting the bridge and crossing the street towards a large monastery. Diego figured that building must be what he was looking for. He followed after them and was soon at the reception desk. Behind the desk was a tubby, old-looking monk. He barely tilted his fat chin up to look at Diego.

Diego asked, "*Señor*, a bed please."

"There are none left," snapped the man.

Diego sighed wearily. "Really? It looks a big place."

Momentarily the man squinted at Diego before he half-cocked his head towards a map on the adjacent wall. Yellow dots emphasised the main Camino Portugués paths, however there were also blue dots of another pilgrimage, mainly following the dots of the Camino, but branching off somewhere closer to Lisbon. "Did you not notice on the way, the blue arrows of Fátima pointing in the opposite direction to your walk?"

"Er, no?" Diego scrutinised the map.

"Hmm, you know in Portugal the most popular Camino is not to Santiago de Compostela?"

"No, I didn't know that," said Diego as his stomach grumbled and his patience began to wear.

"Camino de Fátima is our Camino. And we must hold back some beds for those who make that pilgrimage."

"Oh?" was all Diego could think to say in response.

"Although, we can offer you space on the floor of our dormitory, and we can rent you a mattress."

"I'll take that, then."

"Six euros, and fill out your details there," said the man flicking a finger at a ledger. "You can find your mattress in the dormitory, a volunteer will show you there."

The monk called towards an adjoining room and an elderly man with a slightly crooked stance appeared. Diego completed the ledger and left the money on the desk, and the aged volunteer led him courteously along several long corridors to the dormitory. On the way, Diego noticed some framed poems on the wall and the name of one of them caught his attention: *Dark Night of the Soul* and passing by it he read a few of its lines:

> *Without other light or guide*
> *Save that which in my heart was burning.*
> *That light guided me*
> *More surely than the noonday sun*

They arrived at a large but cramped room of pilgrims making camp on the floor. The room was hot and sticky. Slanted in a corner were tatty foam mattresses. There was still some floor space beside a large window overlooking steel railings and the street. The volunteer nodded towards the mattresses, mentioning that the bathroom was back along the corridor. If he was lucky, there might still be some hot water left. Diego put his pack down beside the window and grimaced as soon as he felt the texture of the mattress, which reminded him of cheap toilet paper. He looked at the other pilgrims, attempting to sense their moods. Some had the look of hippies, others students, and in the main, they were generally younger than himself, apart from a group of French retirees.

Everyone was organising themselves without too much fuss. Diego turned his attention back to the window and above the railings he noticed that the moon was now visible. It was a watery pale blue, but it was full and appeared bright, and it gave him an idea.

He returned the mattress, grabbed his backpack and found the bathroom along the corridor. He didn't spend long in there but was grateful that the shower water had remained hot. He dried himself off with his shirt and put on his new soccer shirt. Glancing in the mirror he grinned as he admired the Lion badge on his chest, thinking that Arnau back home would not have approved of his new shirt. Remembering that Sporting Lisbon was where the great Portuguese footballer, Cristiano Ronaldo, had begun his career. He'd become most famous at Real Madrid, and thus a constant thorn in the side of his and Arnau's team Barcelona, scoring many times against them when the two great football clubs met. Until this Camino, Diego had barely given Arnau and Bar Paradiso a second thought. He hoped he was still running the bar with his same frank opinions and finely tuned wet cloth, with which he targeted at flies.

Diego put his jacket on, but before leaving the monastery poked his head into the office. He ignored the monk's irritable glance and peeked at the wall map. It confirmed that upstream the river did indeed intersect the Central Camino at the town of Ponte de Lima.

DETOUR

Outside it was now dusk, and in the cooling air, Diego shivered under his hat. Although, he remained stead-fast in his plan to follow the river upstream and walk through the night. The shower had restored his energy and he felt confident this detour would help him gain a couple of days, and that soon he'd be enjoying the paths of the Central. As long as he upped his pace, he should arrive in Santiago just in time for their wedding anniversary. Along the street towards the bridge, he noticed the fluorescent sign of a kebab take-away and headed towards it. Next door there was also a tobacconist and Diego immediately remembered he'd run out of smokes.

With a kebab and tobacco tin in hand, Diego strolled towards the moonlit river. When he'd finished eating, he rolled himself a cigarette. It was low tide and the river was silent. Nonetheless, looking downstream, Diego could see dark volumes of water spiralling strongly towards its ocean destination. *I'm also on my way again*, he thought as he smoked his roll-up and reached inside his jacket for his hip flask.

Paving and a road followed the river's route upstream. At the point the river diverged from the road, a sandy track made a path through marshy scrubland towards stilted structures silhouetted against the greying sky. Some of the ancient quays appeared just as stumps, having fallen into the river, though there were occasional vessels anchored to the more intact ones. Diego gave them a cursory look and pressed on. A kilometre or so further upstream, the river turned sharply and Diego's path came to a halt at a gate. The marshland appeared to stretch much further away from the river, creating different channels of water and lagoons. Diego heard a fish jump in the closest pool. He leaned on the gate and viewed the expanse of glistening water, extending outwards into the darkness, beyond which he could see grey ridges above the river.

The land was an unblemished, remote place. Diego smoked another roll-up and contemplated the navigable conditions. As he saw it, his options were to go back and steal one of those little boats, climb the gate and try to cross the waterways, or follow a new track, which was no more than a ribbon of worn dirt running alongside the high brush leading away from the river.

His thinking led him to follow the narrow track. After a while it brought him to a crossroads of chalky pathways, one of which led to a subway under a concrete bridge carrying a highway. A car thudded across the bridge and the light from its headlamps briefly revealed graffiti on the concrete slabs supporting the bridge, where the usual profanities and declarations of love were sprawled. However, Diego could have sworn he saw a mural of a fireman holding a watering can over the smouldering figure of a guitarist, wearing a wide-brimmed Stetson with the words: *EL RELÁMPAGO CHUPA*. Diego approached the subway and strained his eyes but the moonlight didn't enter the space.

He flicked his lighter and held up its flame to the concrete. He hadn't been mistaken; the mural was emblazoned with the words of, "El Relámpago sucks". Then he smelled the freshly sprayed paint. Diego swayed, but caught his balance by placing his right hand on his hip and widening his stance to steady himself. Doing so, he glimpsed his shadow stretching across the opposite wall and found himself admiring his flickering outline. It was a strange feeling; his name was being slandered and yet he liked this gritty outlaw shadow of himself.

He put his lighter in a pocket and passed under the highway, hoping the track would lead to a road that would resume its path along the course of the river. He felt hopeful of this when he crossed a small footbridge over what he figured was a tributary of the main river, and he soon arrived on the outskirts of another town. In the town he could ask someone and regroup, he figured. But it was sparse and everything was shuttered up for the night. So he continued along a road leading out of the town.

The moon was high and lit the country road well, but Diego needed more encouragement to carry on much further. Without his phone and mapping app, he was beginning to doubt his pilgrim instincts. Plus, he felt his backpack cutting into his shoulders and he was tiring. He paused and reaching a hand down, kneaded his sagging belly. He pushed on, hugging the edge of the asphalt road for fear of a speeding car coming his way, while remaining alert for flashes of headlights ahead.

Further on he passed a closed garage, but soon after arrived at another roadside village and he noticed a bus shelter beside a *pastelaria*. Diego could see there were no lights on in the café, but regardless, he peeked through its lattice grill and its window. The shadowy interior reminded him of late nights in Bar Paradiso. He could make out the dark wedge of a lengthy counter, with tapas-style cabinets on its top, and a tall glass fridge lit one corner of the room. He would have killed for a cold *caña* right now. He had to give

Arnau credit: his draught beers were always icy cold, what-ever the time of day.

He removed his hands from the metal and turned back to face the road, glancing up at the midnight moon. It had now arched across the sky, but he had no idea in which direction it was moving and whether its path across the sky would help with his navigation. Besides, he didn't feel like walking any further and he needed to sleep. Diego growled under his breath, angry at the prospect of possibly having to backtrack and annoyed at himself for many other things, too. He inspected the bus timetable on the shelter. Thankfully he was on the right road, as there was a bus to Ponte de Lima. However, the next bus wasn't until nine the next morning.

Reluctant as he was to catch a bus, he told himself that technically he wasn't on the Camino and this was a kind of digression, a branch in his road; thereafter, he would continue to walk the paths of the Camino. There was nothing else to do but unroll his sleeping bag and attempt to get some sleep under the shelter. The wooden bench was too short to sleep on so Diego placed his bag on the paving beside it. The ground was hard, yet he managed to sleep and a dream strayed into his mind.

It took him back to a time he and Mari weren't married and they had visited Seville for a long weekend. They had wanted to enjoy flamenco as the audience did, as spectators, experiencing that profound feeling of *duende* that the best flamenco artists could impress upon you. And Seville was one of the places to find that. For a brief period during their first evening there, they had got separated in Barrio de Santa Cruz, the old quarter, as their curiosities had distracted them, leading them in different directions.

In the dream, Diego was wandering blindly along a labyrinth of cobbled lanes, turning his head from side to side and ducking around people. He called out, "Mari," but no one responded to that name, or cared to look towards where his shouting was coming from. He walked and walked, aimlessly passing people like a ghost until he found himself in a busy plaza, where residents gazed down from their apartment balconies above the bars and restaurants.

Their attention was drawn to a group of men around a bar table. Two of them had guitars resting in their laps. The men laughed and made fun of each other, and when they finished their beers, the guitarists strummed their guitar strings, and the others cupped their hands together. The oldest, a dark-haired and broad-chested man, rose from his chair and a *cante*, a flamenco song, echoed around the square. Their flamenco always seemed to sense the audience's mood and each of their songs was rewarded with a flutter of coins. They'd raise their arms, cry, '*¡Olé!*,' and then order another round of drinks.

Diego had positioned himself against a sherry barrel outside a bar called Casa de Luthier, observing the men and their music. Occasionally mists of spray from table parasols wafted his way, cooling his face in the warm summer night's air, and it was at this point his dream merged with images from his Camino. Mari was dancing through a hazy forest and Diego was sitting against the trunk of an enormous cedar, his legs straddled in front of him, with the branches of the tree fanning him in the wind. Mari was barely visible but Diego recognised it was her from the summer dress she was wearing and the mist wisping around her high-arched feet. Then the fog thickened and she was gone. Occasionally he'd hear her footsteps padding across the forest floor. A car zoomed through the village, arousing Diego from the dream. He slept fitfully thereafter. But each time Diego awoke he felt a breeze, and it comforted him to think of distant cedars bending in the wind.

He heard the dawn chorus of singing birds and he peeked at his watch. It was just after six and the chill a reminder that autumn was fast approaching. Briefly, he closed his eyes again, thinking there were still a few hours until the bus would arrive. However, the rattling of shutters beckoned his attention. Diego sat upright and looked over his shoulder, yawning.

"Care for some breakfast?" asked a middle-aged woman, who was wearing a bright floral dress and holding a padlock in her hand.

Diego's yawning face curled into a smile. "*¡Claro! señora.*"

"Well, help me with this blasted shutter; it's always getting stuck!"

Diego jumped out of his bag, swiftly pulled on his shoes and stepped over to the metal grill. He placed a hand on the latch where the padlock had just been, gave it a little shake and pulled it back with ease.

"How did you do that?" remarked the woman.

"I've had a lot of doors close on me in the past!" he quipped. The woman continued to look perplexed. "Um, what I meant to say was I've worked in a couple of bars and these grills are always the same when they get old. A good shake always works."

The woman removed a key from her shoulder bag and Diego gathered up his things from the bus stand. "Before you leave you can show me this shaking technique again," said the woman as she led Diego into the café.

"Sure," replied Diego as he followed her inside.

She turned the lights on and reached out a hand. "I'm Teresa."

"Diego," he responded, shaking her hand and noticing on the walls scarves and photos dedicated to Porto Football Club.

Teresa turned the coffee machine on and Diego went into the bathroom. When he returned, the place was already starting to fill up. He found himself a space at the end of the bar and climbed onto a stool. Teresa was serving a customer but she glanced towards Diego and asked, "Coffee?"

"Absolutely," he replied, removing his hat. "*Café solo* please."

By the time Diego was onto his second black coffee the *pastelaria* was humming with the usual sorts he might have expected to find in a café-cum-bar in rural Spain. There were the farmers and labourers gathered around the long side of the bar, rebutting each other, though here it was mostly done with a smile; elderly gentlemen passing the morning newspapers around; retired women enjoying a friendly gossip and a pastry. But also fathers and mothers dropped in for a few minutes to buy *doces*, sweets for their kids on the way to school, and as an excuse to say hello. This wasn't the first time he'd noticed this more tranquil, convivial way of life in Portugal. They appeared united; it was like they realised they needed each other in their community.

It was still early, but already Teresa was chalking up the menu of the day onto the A-board. Diego immediately obliged and was soon enjoying a plate of French fries and *francesinha*, a toasted sandwich stuffed with sausage and meat and oozing with melted cheese. Given its weightiness, Diego decided he should wash it down with a glass of the straw-coloured wine that most of the men were drinking. It was cool and took the edge off the morning.

When it was soon time to catch the bus, an elderly-woman breezed through the doors. She was slim, and her wrinkled skin was yellowing. Diego slid off his stool and shouldered his pack. Immediately Teresa came from around the counter, and joining them both by the door said to Diego, "This is my mother, Cassandra." Cassandra maintained steady eye contact with Diego and smiled as he stretched out his arm towards her.

"Nice to meet you, I'm Diego," he said shaking her coarse hand.

"Diego has a knack for shutters," explained Teresa to her mother.

The women stepped outside with Diego and he again demonstrated his technique in front of them. When he was done Cassandra said, "Hmm, not so many practical young men around these days."

Diego half-smiled at her, accepting the praise, but wondering how practical was he really, given this was a modern world and he had just given up all of his music royalties. He reassured himself by thinking Mari would understand.

Cassandra continued, "Funny, your fingers were hard, but your palm is very soft." Again her eyes rested on Diego as the bus arrived. Diego wished them both well and boarded the stairs of the bus.

Cassandra yelled hoarsely, "*Guapo*, handsome!" Diego looked over his shoulder as he ascended the steps of the bus and she said, "That's a funny shirt to be wearing for a flamenco guitarist." Diego found a smile creeping into the corners of his mouth, but he remained tight-lipped and shook off her comment with a wave of his strumming hand. The pistons of the door hissed, and the bus pulled away.

THE FOREST CLIMB

The time Diego had gained by arriving on the Central Camino path, he'd lost by catching up on his sleep in Ponte de Lima. He now estimated it would take around a week to walk to Santiago, but his wedding anniversary was in five days. Still, the mist was rising from the valley and the path felt good underfoot. Plus, his new companions, Paul and Thomas, two youthful Germans whom he'd met at the stone-built *albergue* in Ponte de Lima, were also up for walking two of the stages today. So Diego was feeling positive that he could make up the ground.

It would be nearly forty kilometres to Tui, and first there was the challenge of climbing the steepest ascent on the Central to a pass in the mountain ridges, before pushing into the Coura valley beyond. The three walkers spread out across the wide path with Diego's backpack appearing smallish relative to the stuffed backpacks of his new friends. Between them, the Germans carried a tent and thick army-style sleeping bags amongst other things. Their routine had been to alternate between hostel and campsite.

They communicated in English and Diego learned both of the Germans were midway through university and this was their big summer adventure. Thomas was the larger of the two and more confident. Paul, being much shorter and with dark features, appeared more Italian than German to Diego. And he couldn't picture him studying high finance. The friends had met on the same economics degree course in Berlin. The richer of the celebrities Diego had rubbed shoulders with seemed to have a habit of talking about money and investing, almost to the point of obsession. It was something that had never interested him much. But with the two Germans chattering between themselves about MBAs, internships, trading and getting your foot in the door with the big banks, Diego had found himself interjecting and asking, "Man, where's the fire? What's the rush with your careers?"

"A fat salary and a Porsche parked in my driveway before I'm twenty-five. Wouldn't that be sweet?" replied Thomas.

Diego immediately responded, "Can't say I miss my Merc."

"What is it you do?" asked Paul eying Diego.

"I'm a musician. But in my time I've learned to change a beer barrel, pick grapes – and some other things too."

Thomas smirked. "A credit card plugs the gaps."

Diego thought for a moment, and answered, "Hmm, maybe, but I actually enjoy changing a guitar string, and learning to do things for myself." He glanced into the dense forest they were passing through, observing that a few of the leaves on the trees were already yellowing and browning. Then he looked back at the Germans and remarked, "Being reliant on others for money isn't always a good thing."

They passed a couple walking the pilgrimage together and Thomas gestured back at them, before glancing at Diego. "Try telling that to your Mrs when you've got no money."

Diego didn't respond; Thomas' comment had jarred slightly, as the thought crossed his mind that Mari might not initially understand why he'd so readily handed over his royalties to Mark. But more importantly, he needed confirmation that she'd arrive in Santiago to coincide with their wedding anniversary. All being well, he would be able to check his emails that night in Tui and find out. His mind began to wander further and he thought about some of the things he might say to Mari in Santiago. Perhaps having a child together might be the answer to their problems?

The path rounded a stream, and as they followed it uphill, Diego noticed Paul was slightly dragging a leg. "Paul, you're limping?"

"It's nothing," he replied feigning a smile.

Thomas marched on ahead and a few minutes later they passed through the hamlet of a stone chapel and café-cum-convenience store. Diego stopped and yelled after Thomas. "Hold on, I need a coffee and to buy some water."

Thomas came to an abrupt halt and turned half round, scrutinising the situation. In a commanding tone, he shouted back. "Well, okay, if you're thirsty. But after, we should hike up to the pass in one go."

They grabbed an outside table and Paul rolled down the sock of his sore leg. There was some swelling around his ankle.

"I have an idea," said Thomas. "We should order some ice with our drinks."

Paul nodded and they ordered coffees and iced water. Thomas wrapped the ice cubes from the water in the keffiyeh he'd been wearing around his neck and pressed it against Paul's ankle.

Relaxing, Paul smiled and took hold of the improvised icepack. "Well, as we'll be here for a little while, let me share with you a story about another determined man." Paul raised his coffee cup at Thomas and continued talking, "I was reading a story in the local newspaper in Ponte de Lima and if I interpreted it correctly, it went something like this."

Diego raised an eyebrow. "You're learning Portuguese?"

"Thought I'd give it a go… whilst I'm here in Portugal."

"Cigarette, boys?" asked Diego preparing to settle in for the story.

Both of the Germans politely shook their heads. Diego began rolling his smoke, whilst Thomas grumbled under his breath, knowing his friend's stories could be on the lengthy side.

Paul began recalling the story. "They have a strange custom in Ponte de Lima, known as the Vaca das Cordas. Every year the day before Corpus Christi they tie a bull to the iron grille of the bell tower of the parish church with a long rope. Then they make the bull run around the tower three times."

"… Hmm, what's the point of that?" quizzed Thomas.

"…I don't know. Anyway, afterwards, the local bakers lead the bull through the streets in a huge procession to the main square. The square is covered with sand and all the alleyways and exits are barricaded off. Arriving, the bull is tormented into a frenzy and then released into the square. By then many in the town are drunk and exuberant and the craziest of the men scatter into the square and jostle with the bull.

"But this year, one young man ran into the temporary bullring ahead of the others. Holding a red cape he announced to the crowd, and his on-watching girlfriend, that he would like to marry her and he would fight the bull until she said yes. She didn't respond, perhaps dumbstruck at the proposal. The bull charged the man, but he didn't turn quick enough, and its horn scraped across his arm, drawing blood. *'Olé, Olé'!'* cried the men in the crowd, with the bull looking on in confusion at the impromptu matador. The man yelled again towards his girlfriend imploring her to say 'yes,' and get him out of the situation of his own making, but she remained silent. The women in the crowd screamed at the girlfriend too, but to no avail either. So the *matador* took a deep breath, pushed out his chest and again flicked his cape at the bull.

"Everyone cheered now, including the women, and the bull lowered its head and charged the man. Again the man was too slow with his pass, but this time the bull tossed him into the air. The young man landed on his back and didn't move. With that, officials jumped in with whips and rope to secure the bull, and medics went to treat the boyfriend; he was okay, just bruised. As they stretchered him out he sat upright and looked towards his girlfriend with his arms open wide. The paper said the silence was deafening as the crowd awaited her answer."

"Did she…?" asked Thomas.

"Can you believe it – she said no!" replied Paul.

"No way!" said Thomas glancing at Diego.

"*¡Madre mía!*" exclaimed Diego.

Paul shrugged his shoulders. "Then a brass band played and they released the bull again. At that point, all the drunken men swarmed around it."

Diego grinned and raised his index fingers to his Stetson, imitating bullhorns, and prodded his head towards Paul. "Hey, you want to be a *toreador*, or perhaps even a matador." He sprang up and then grabbed the shirt that he'd tied to the back of his backpack. He cast it in front of his torso and flicking it towards Paul, said, "*¡Olé, Olé!*"

Paul and Thomas laughed. They finished their drinks, and Paul assured them that the ice had relieved his ankle. So they shouldered their backpacks, feeling ready to tackle the climb ahead. The path steepened as they entered a forest of pines. Suddenly, a pinecone bounced off the crown of Diego's hat, directing him to look further into the woodland. Studying the trees, he noticed sap being drawn from the pines into plastic bags, and there were patches where trees had been felled and cleared. Immediately he was reminded of Leonardo, his brother from his first Camino and he reflected on how its path had helped Leonardo 'discover' his purpose, which was to work with trees. Leonardo had spoken with much enthusiasm about the contributions that the various trees make to the planet.

It wasn't long after that Diego had committed to his own purpose too, the flamenco guitar. It now seemed so long ago, yet here he was now walking away from the guitar. But he reassured himself by thinking he would find his purpose with Mari in Santiago. All he had to do was get there in time for their anniversary – arriving by foot, she would see his determination to make amends.

They continued to push hard up the path and much of Diego's focus was on planting each of his heavy steps up the steep hill. He pulled his pack in closer as Paul dropped further behind them. After a while, Paul was out of sight and Thomas turned and yelled down the path, "You alright, Paul?"

Through the trees they heard Paul shouting back, "I'm okay, keep going."

Thomas paused and turned to Diego. "*Nein!* It's my fault, I've been pushing him too hard."

Diego squinted as the sun broke through the treeline and he caught his breath, "Shit happens," he said over his shoulder as he pushed on up the hill. His Stetsoned silhouette looked like a pitiless scar cut into the sun.

Wheezing, Diego arrived at the mountain pass and reached for his bottle of water. By the time Thomas joined him, Diego had switched to drinking from his hip flask. Diego shook his flask towards Thomas.

"I assume it's not water?"

Diego smirked. "Some call it the water of life."

Thomas nodded and reached for the flask. He took just a small sip, but it was still enough to contort his face. Noticing, Diego responded by saying, "It'll put hairs on your chest, *amigo.*"

They didn't say anything else as they looked out across the canopy of pines and waited for Paul to join them. The valley below, where they had begun their day's walk, distracted their thoughts. The scattered dwellings below the blue mountains appeared lost to Diego. It was only the distant echoes of the Sunday church bells that hinted they weren't detached from the rest of humanity. Paul soon arrived and immediately Thomas handed his friend some water.

Taking the bottle, Paul gestured towards the clearing behind them, where there was a small caravan selling snacks and beers, with pilgrims sitting around a couple of fold-up tables in the shade. "I need to take a break," he said, before he drank thirstily from the bottle.

Thomas grinned. "Our reward!"

Diego nodded, adjusting the brim of his Stetson over his brow. "Definitely. Especially as werewolves shouldn't be in the sun for too long."

"Werewolves?" said Paul.

"The Portuguese words painted above the hatch are very similar to Spanish. They say The Werewolf Bar," Diego said over his shoulder as he walked towards the caravan. His mood lifting, he shrilled a coyote calling of "*Ayeeee…*" in his best gypsy high-pitched tone. As he did, he found himself thinking of Camarón de la Isla and the stories of his late-night performances at the Andalucían festivals.

They ordered hamburgers and beers and joined an Irishman who was walking the Camino with his grown-up daughter. The silver-haired father mentioned he'd sworn the whole way up the tough climb. The blonde daughter smiled fondly at her father and said, "Da, you're doing very well." Everyone around the table was in a good mood; Thomas and Paul didn't mind the jokes directed at the Germans, about their precision and complicated language. Diego stretched out his aching limbs, loosened his shoes and rolled a cigarette. Soon he was gesturing at everyone for another beer; he discovered his new companions were ready to continue walking, but he easily persuaded Thomas and Paul, leaning on their masculine insecurities and quipping, "Aren't the Germans meant to be expert drinkers?"

Diego would have sat there drinking all afternoon and into the night had the owner of the beer caravan not announced he was closing up. Nonetheless, Diego took a nip of his whisky and offered some to Thomas and Paul, slurring, "For the road," as he stood up, steadying himself with a hand on the table. Thomas obliged but Paul passed on the whisky; checking the mapping application on his phone, he said, "We've still got around 25 kilometres of walking left."

Diego sighed as he glanced at the stony path of the Camino, perforated by the shadows of the upper boughs of the pines. "Well, at least it's downhill for a while."

Thomas glanced at Paul. "Is the ankle good?"

"*Ja*, it feels okay now. And there's only one small hill left today."

They descended the hill and when it flattened out the Germans set a good pace. Diego felt the trail taking its toll on his knees, although he marched alongside them, determined to reach Tui that night and make his Santiago deadline. They maintained the pace but when they paused to drink some water, Diego began to relax a little and felt comfortable dropping behind. Conversation felt arduous relative to the physical exertion, plus he wanted to think about his pending meeting with Mari. He guessed by now she would have responded to his email, and he felt hopeful about his proposal of meeting in time for their anniversary.

Before too long, the path turned and dropped down to an ancient Roman bridge with large flagstones. Diego couldn't see the Germans and he upped his pace towards the crossing. However, when he got there, he felt a headache coming on and paused, pressing his hands against the side of the ancient bridge. The stones were still warm. Stretching his head to look over the wall, his Stetson loosened from around his crown and fell into the stream below. In the twilight, he couldn't see where his hat had landed, but weariness overpowered his immediate desire to chase after it, and he continued to rest at the bridge.

The only sounds he heard were his shallow breaths and the water lapping over stones. He reached for his flask and drank the remains of his whisky, then he went down to the riverbank. His hat had washed up on some scree and was within easy reach. He retrieved it, and as it was already sodden, he scooped up some water and proceeded to tip his hat over his head. He shook himself down, rejoined the Camino path and ploughed on walking.

The Germans were waiting patiently for Diego at a late-night café in the centre of Valença, just off the Camino trail. They were sitting outside at a table and drinking coffee. Diego arrived exhausted and observing Valença was a large town with several hotels, made his mind up to stay the night in the town. He set his pack against the table, sat down and began rolling himself a cigarette.

"Do you want a coffee?" asked Paul.

"Thanks, but no thanks," replied Diego. "I'm calling it quits and will stay here the night."

"Tui's not that much further. Just a kilometre or two, a bridge to cross, and then we'll be there and in Spain," offered Paul.

Thomas raised his coffee cup at Diego. "*Amigo*, we can drink a bottle of Spanish wine together and toast our arrival in your homeland."

Diego shook his head, his attention drawn to an upmarket hotel across the street. The thought of soft bed sheets was already on his mind, although he was also aware that the hotel would likely have a guest computer, and he urgently needed to check his emails. He looked back at the Germans. "I'll make an early start in the morning."

The Germans gave up trying to persuade Diego – they could see he had resolved to stay in Valença – and they departed with friendly handshakes. Diego finished smoking his cigarette as he watched the Germans marching towards a cobbled alleyway leading through the historical centre and in the direction of the bridge. He stubbed out his cigarette, shouldered his pack and crossed the street to the hotel.

NORTHERN LIGHTS

A shower and then sleep was on Diego's mind as soon as he checked in to the hotel, however there was still an important thing to do first. He sat down at the guest computer in the lobby and logged into his email account. There were two emails from Gracia, the first one he read confirmed that Mark had received the contract signing over Diego's royalties exclusively to him. Diego didn't bother reading her most recent email because the email he'd been hoping to see had just arrived in his account – it was from Mari.

He opened it and the first words he saw were: *Lo siento,* I'm sorry. Immediately Diego understood Mari would not be joining him in Santiago for their wedding anniversary. Diego shuddered, feeling like he'd been stung all over. His next thought was to reach for his whisky, but he remembered he'd finished it off earlier at the bridge. He read the email from the beginning:

Dear Diego,
I hope you're enjoying your Portuguese Camino.

I've been trying to call you but you didn't answer your phone – perhaps your battery is dead? I wanted to talk to you but I will have to write to you instead.

As we haven't been able to talk of late, I haven't been able to tell you how I'm feeling. To be honest, I was a little lonely in the hotel at first, and I was finding it difficult to let go. Not only because I didn't want to hurt you, but also because I can't deny that there isn't something between us. But deep down, I know you will never change. For example, as soon as I suggested we should meet, you started saying the same old thing, which you once thought I wanted to hear, that we could travel together. Then you started placing demands on me, taking a mile when I offered an inch – rushing when we meet up, in time for our anniversary. Mentioning we might renew our wedding vows, as if everything was okay between us! It all felt too much and I began wondering if I had done the right thing by suggesting we meet in Santiago.

And on top of all of that, you said you'd given away your royalties to Marco. That was our security, and you didn't even think to consult me first! Though perhaps it was a good thing, because it showed me once and for all how selfish you are. And, truth be told, I haven't been missing you these past few days, and already I'm starting to relax in my own company. I've made a couple of nice friends and they're all I need right now. Actually, there doesn't seem to be a day that goes by when I don't have some kind of wonderful interaction with somebody. So we can't meet up. Lo siento, it was wrong of me to even consider it. I think it's best I stay here for a little longer.

It's finally time to accept that we have no future together and to put a line in the sand – for the sake of both of us. Deep down I think you're not sure about us either. If you were, you wouldn't have behaved how you have – maybe you want to set yourself free too. Tomorrow I will definitely contact a lawyer to apply for a divorce.

Please don't come to San Sebastian and try and find me, as you won't be able to persuade me to change my mind. I hope we can both find what we are looking for.

Mari

Diego felt sick, yet he still wanted a drink. He logged out of his email account and followed the sign to the bar. It was dimly lit and devoid of customers. A barman was closing off the beer taps. None of that mattered as Diego eyed the array of liquor bottles lining the bar shelving behind the barman. His eyes soon landed on one of the bottles.

Leaning his pack against a chair and gesturing towards the bottle, he said, "A large Jack Daniels."

"*Senhor*, the bar is now closed," replied the barman.

"Hmm, I'll buy the bottle and take it to my room then. You can sell it to me?"

Momentarily the barman paused as he thought over the request and sensed Diego was already a little drunk, but there was no denying his dark eyes. "Of course, I will arrange for room service to take it up to your room with some ice."

THE BREEZE from the Miño River ruffled Diego's hair as he sat outside on the balcony of his top-floor room, drinking a Jack Daniels. He could see the pale lights of Tui, in Spain, on the distant hills beyond Valença and river dividing the two countries. But that didn't matter. There was nothing left. He knew his marriage and this journey were over. He also knew he was drunk, but he continued to drink, now not bothering to top up his whiskey tumbler, instead drinking directly from the bottle.

He told himself he would take a shower when he'd finished the bottle. Persuading himself he was a legendary drinker, and whatever happened it was the one thing he could control. Drink was the companion that would never let him down. Perhaps he'd stay in the hotel for several days; this would be his rock-star swansong. After all, he had an AMEX, and he might as well enjoy it, as Dan had suggested. It was a comfortable hotel, plus the barman asked no questions.

Diego placed a hand on the rail of the balcony, pulled himself to his feet and leaned over as he pondered the idea some more. He slouched into the railings; his legs like jelly as he adjusted his gaze and attempted to focus on the distant lights. From somewhere deep inside he still felt the need to walk, but he needed an idea, a reason – a purpose to compel him to keep walking. He dragged over a chair and climbed onto it. He was wobbly but he managed to maintain his balance as he attempted to get a better look at the faraway lights of Spain. They smudged into a single trail and he gazed at them hopefully, but his mind remained bereft. He bent down and stretched out his strumming hand towards the whisky bottle he'd left on the nearby table. In that same moment the chair slid from beneath him and he fell backwards over the balcony.

Diego's body slammed hard onto the roof of the hotel's porch and he rolled over its edge and into the swimming pool below it, where he sank quickly. The wind picked up and shadows from the surrounding palm trees swayed over the pool like shards of glass.

PART II

THE VIEW OF THE BRIDGE

Diego opened his eyes and gazed through the open shutters and past the Juliet balcony at what was now becoming a familiar vista. His view was of a metal bridge spanning the Miño River. Squinting, he tried to focus on the opposite bank at the medieval town of Tui spread over several green hills. Fleetingly, he cast his eyes above the town's hilltop cathedral to clouds streaked orange-rose.

Diego cursed inwardly. He'd lost track of what day it was, but the doctor had told him he might expect his headaches to last for at least three weeks. This was the first morning that his head wasn't aching, so he suspected he'd been convalescing at Brahim's guesthouse for at least three weeks now. He made a mental note to ask Brahim what day it was when he saw him. But if he had been recovering for three weeks, it meant he would likely have to stay for another five weeks. The doctor had also said it would take him a minimum of eight weeks to recover from fracturing his pelvis – as long as he took things slowly, and gently rebuilt the physical strength in his leg. But at least he was now able to shuffle to the bathroom without the aid of the walking frame the hospital had given him.

In the early morning light, the room had a pinkish glow from the sun brightening the apricot-tinged plastered walls. Above, the wooden beams of the old house were exposed, giving the room extra height, yet it still felt cosy. Two Moroccan rugs ran across the tiled floor, dividing the room. On one side was the dining area, with a small table and two chairs, their backs upholstered in mossy green. Against one of the adjacent walls was a divan with colourful silk cushions. A wide hallway ran from the bedroom leading to the kitchenette and the bathroom.

Diego glanced blankly into the tall mirror on the sidewall beside the bed before he looked back at Spain. He remained stunned by his recent change of circumstances. On top of the concussion and breaking his pelvis, owing all that tax had left him penniless. Furthermore, he wasn't sure if he could pay for his enforced stay at the guesthouse. More cruel, however, was the feeling of being alone again. When he had arrived at the guesthouse the divorce papers had been waiting for him. Thinking Mari would want to be at Diego's side, Gracia had informed her of his fall and had given her the address of the guesthouse. Mari had not joined him. Angry, confused, and perhaps still under the influence of the oxycodone, Diego had immediately signed the papers and asked Brahim to post them.

With his memory fully restored, Diego played back in his mind his recent discoveries and the events that had led him to where he currently lay.

~

DIEGO HAD BEEN LUCKY, very lucky. Falling, his body had twisted mid-flight, and he had smashed into the porch on his left side, his hip and buttock areas absorbing most of the impact. The high porch roof had reduced the full impact and the swimming pool was a kinder surface to fall on than the paving stones. A quick-minded diner in the hotel's restaurant had been fast to react upon hearing Diego crashing into the pool. He had jumped up from his table and dragged Diego out of the pool. Drowning is what would have killed him. He was still breathing at that point, although unconscious. But this state had been short-lived, and by the time the ambulance had taken him to the private hospital in Valença, he had regained consciousness.

The doctor examining Diego had diagnosed him of having a mild concussion, but he was more worried about his hip. However, the x-ray revealed he had sustained a pelvic fracture, which wouldn't require surgery. The break would cure naturally with some gentle exercise and plenty of rest. The oxycodone the nurse had given Diego helped him sleep through the night, and the next day had been able to borrow a phone and call Gracia.

On hearing the news, Gracia's first reaction was to immediately drop everything and join Diego at the hospital. But sensing Diego was unaware of his financial predicament, the situation of which she had stated in her latest email, she figured he must know immediately he was in serious financial trouble. A fact that had only come to light after Diego had relinquished all of his royalty rights to Mark.

Gracia explained that for several months, Mark had been under investigation by the tax authorities in Madrid for not declaring all of his income, as well as his clients' incomes. The authorities had discovered he'd been hiding the money in companies registered in low-tax foreign jurisdictions. As a result, Diego was facing big fines for tax evasion, not to mention having to immediately pay a large outstanding sum of tax. As the orchestrator of the tax fraud, Mark was possibly facing a prison sentence. Fortunately, Diego's accountant was able to prove that Diego never had any understanding of his financial affairs. The accountant wasn't to blame either, because he'd always declared any income Diego generated in

Spain. Thus the accountant's only crime was ignorance of what was happening to some of Diego's income at a higher level. Diego's full tax liability would be close to two million euros.

Despite Diego's groggy state, he had realised his only option to cover the debt would be to sell his penthouse, the Mercedes, and any of his other assets that would bring in money fast. So Diego had asked Gracia to liaise with his accountant to arrange that. It was at this point that he told Gracia about Mari and their marriage, adding that she should tell the accountant to pass any remaining funds over to Mari. In his injured condition Diego no longer had the energy or will to try and sway Mari to remain with him. Besides, he couldn't be with anyone now. What could he offer? He was a worthless drunk. He hated who he was and what he had become. He didn't even want to be in his own company. And so, he was adamant that Gracia shouldn't fly out to be with him.

By day two, Diego was determined to leave the hospital. The clinicians were fine about his departure but had cautioned him that his mobility would be limited and had provided him with a walking frame, urging him not to travel far and to convalesce in one place for at least a couple of weeks. Diego had agreed that he needed Gracia to help him find somewhere nearby and affordable to stay. She'd searched online, and that's how Diego came to be staying in the small apartment that could accommodate disabled guests, at the recently refurbished 19th-century guesthouse in Valença.

From the window, Diego felt the September air on his cheeks and it dawned on him that autumn had already arrived. Wincing, he cautiously drew his legs towards his chest, swivelled slowly in the bed and lowered his limbs to the floor.

Placing his palms on the mattress, he tentatively got out of bed, steadying himself with his hands. Diego took a deep breath then slowly made his way towards the corridor, resting a hand on the walking frame, before pushing it away. He paused in front of the mirror to examine his bruising. Pulling the left side of his boxers down revealed his left hip area was still bruised, although it was now turning a lighter shade of brown. His limbs continued to urge him to walk. Diego reached with his left hand for the handrail running the length of the corridor and progressively made his way towards the bathroom.

POCO A POCO

Diego stepped outside, steadying himself against the railing of the wooden balcony wrapping its way around the interior of the house. The clouds had cleared, the day was bright; aromas of spice filled the air and the stone fountain bubbled in the centre of the courtyard below. Diego had barely left his room since arriving at the guesthouse. He breathed everything in, in one long breath.

The courtyard was decorated with a pebbled mosaic and the whitewashed walls gleamed a brilliant yellowy-white in the sun. Slate tables and metal chairs were dotted around the place, with several divans and antique wooden furniture lining the perimeter. Between the stone pillars supporting the balcony were potted geraniums and fruit trees. Diego noticed a tower section adjoining the main house and realised it had probably been a separate building at one point, appreciating that an inner section of the house must have been knocked out to create this interior garden. Drinking coffee and smoking at a table in the sun suddenly felt very appealing.

Diego tightened his grip on the railing and edged his way towards a corner of the balcony. To his surprise, he made good progress; his leg was tender but no longer throbbed with pain. He rounded the next side of the balcony and steadily headed towards the stairs at the end. However, putting more weight on his injured side on the first step was still not an option. He hovered, pushing damp strands of hair away from his eyes. Slowly he lowered himself into a squat, so eventually he was sitting on the top step. Then he began shuffling down the stairs, using his arms to carry his body forward and down each step. Some five minutes later he was at the bottom and stood up, leaning into a pillar for support. The backs of the chairs helped to steady his balance as he walked towards the sunny table. He pulled out a chair and cautiously sat down.

Diego removed his tobacco from the top pocket of his shirt and began rolling himself a cigarette. Smoking, he tilted an ear towards the fountain and its peaceful gurgles no longer seemed wordless. He couldn't translate it, but the continuous soft flow of the water was nonetheless familiar. His solitude was broken by a friendly voice over his shoulder. Brahim had just come out of the kitchen to smoke. "*Buenos días*, Diego. How are you? Can I get you a coffee and a little something to eat? My treat."

Diego turned to look at the trim man in a denim shirt and mint-coloured chinos. His posture was of someone young and virile, yet his face was quite wrinkled and his hair was like wisps of silver candyfloss. The man smiled gently at Diego as he readjusted the bar towel draped over his shoulder.

"*Gracias*, Brahim that would be excellent. But how's business? You must stop giving me food and drink on the house."

"It's okay, I prepare a lot of food today."

Diego leaned slightly forward. "*Claro*, but has business picked up?"

"I am ever hopeful, Diego."

"Hmm, the summer season must be coming to and end and that means fewer people will be walking the Camino."

"People will come eventually, so every day I must be prepared."

"Well, that's to my advantage, food-wise... but you should be cautious, no?"

"Very much so. But I can't be fearful either, or I will miss opportunities. I have taken precautions, and I have decided to hold off hiring any staff until I see the consistency of trade."

"So you will continue to do all the cooking, cleaning, the bar and everything else yourself?"

Brahim's smile broadened. "Diego, I told you, I like to work."

"I admire your faith," replied Diego, wondering how this man in the autumn years of his life managed to have so much energy, especially as he'd noticed Brahim liked to have a drink too. During Diego's time recuperating at the house, Brahim would check in on him after he had closed up the bar for the night. Often he would bring a bottle of wine and they would chat for a while.

"Okay Diego, I will make your food," said Brahim enthusiastically as he turned and headed back inside. He soon came back with a tray laden with a French press of coffee, olives, bread and hummus. Then he went back to the kitchen.

The food and coffee tasted good outside in the courtyard, and briefly Diego thought of the Camino. But he had no desire to resume it; he had no desire to do anything. Getting better might cause him a problem.

A few minutes later Brahim returned with a glass of wine in hand. "The food is to your satisfaction, Diego?"

"It's excellent. You're a man of many talents, Brahim."

"Thank you, Diego." He gestured to Diego with the wine and placed it on the table.

"Too much!"

Brahim smiled. "A reward for making it down the steps." His wrinkles flattened as he said, "I was thinking of having an antique auction. Do you think this is a good idea?"

Diego took a sip of wine and leaned back into his seat. "An auction?"

"Yes, an auction. I still have many antiques stored in the basement. Having an auction should generate some interest in my place, don't you think?"

"Hmm, perhaps?"

"Will you help me with it, Diego?"

Diego folded his arms across his body and considered his response. "It would raise some money from people that live in the city, but it wouldn't change the fact that most pilgrims prefer to head straight for Tui and end their day's walking across the border in Spain. So I'm not sure how an auction would get you more guests and the pilgrims you had in mind when you created your hotel?"

"Very much so. But I have nothing to lose. Those antiques are gathering dust, and filling this patio with an auction would be fun."

"But how can I help? I know nothing about antiques and I can barely walk, remember!"

"I know some friends who can help with lugging the antiques around and I can take care of the auction itself. I just need someone to help entertain the guests."

"Guests?"

"We will make it an exclusive event."

Diego's arms tightened around his body. "Come on, man! I've battered my pelvis and I'm not sure I'm ready to meet anyone yet."

"Diego, every day you make progress and today you have come down the stairs, step by step unaided. *Poco a poco*, yes? Just like on the Camino. Besides I'm not talking tomorrow... I need a few weeks to spread the word and organise things."

"Brahim, you make a great sales pitch."

Braham smiled again. "But you will think about it?"

Diego gave an approving nod in the direction of the doorway, which led through to the kitchen and bar. "Well, I owe you so much. *Sí*, I will think about it."

"Superb," said Brahim as he patted Diego on the shoulder.

A customer wandered into the courtyard and enquired if the bar was open for lunch. Explaining that it was, Brahim led the customer back to the bar area to show him the menu. Diego began rolling himself another cigarette, his hands shaking with anxiety. *Could I do it?* he thought. *What if someone recognised me? What the hell would I say?* He felt the urge to rest and hide away in his room again. He finished his wine and put his tobacco away, not completing his roll-up. Clenching the arms of his chair, he pulled himself up and slowly made his way back to the foot of the stairs. He sat down on the lower step and began to slowly ascend.

DIEGO DREAMED he was on a wooden bridge strung over a cloud-covered gorge. A strong gale blew, swinging the bridge and making the ropes wail mournful gypsy flamenco *cantes*. Just as he was reaching the other side, plank by plank, the bridge began to give way under his feet. He grabbed at the rope to save himself but it was thin as a guitar string and cut into his hand. He let go and fell weightlessly through the roaring wind. Diego woke up. The *sirocco* wind had blown in while he slept and was violently rattling the shutters on his bedroom window.

Sitting up on the bed he looked out through the window and although his view was a little hazy in the dusk light, he noticed a road barrier had been placed in front of the metal bridge. Observing it further he could see scaffolding had been erected over it. He eased himself off the bed and hobbled over to the window to take a closer look. Casting his eyes down past the balcony rails of his room, he could see cars were being redirected towards the more modern bridge a few kilometres further down the river. The pilgrims would have to cross into Spain at that point too. This meant no business for Brahim. Diego put his shoes on, feeling more concerned than ever for Brahim and his guesthouse.

Diego shuffled outside and in the wind he heard the strains of flamenco music coming from below. He gradually made his way down the stairs and across the courtyard. Opening the door to the bar area revealed that flamenco from the era of Camarón de la Isla and Paco de Lucia was playing through the speakers. Diego went inside and was greeted by enthusiastic chatter. Brahim was behind the long bar, smiling and sweating as he did his best to serve customers. By the look of their walking clothes, Diego figured the majority of them were pilgrims. To his surprise, the closure of the bridge must have resulted in them ending their day's walk in Valença, rather than taking the long detour to the other bridge.

In that moment, Diego discovered his inner bartender, leading him towards the counter. He limped behind it and immediately began filling the glasses of the thirsty pilgrims. Noticing he had help, Brahim dashed into the kitchen. As the night progressed, Diego continued to work the bar whilst Brahim cooked, served the tables and showed guests to rooms.

By midnight the bar and dining areas were clear of people and Brahim lowered the music volume and served them both small draught beers. He urged Diego to take a stool around the other side of the bar.

"How did that feel?" asked Brahim, leaning into the bar.

Diego took a long drink of his beer and replied, "Brahim, I think I have finally discovered my purpose in life."

Brahim laughed. "Well, there's nothing like working up a thirst." He raised his glass towards Diego. "*Santé!*"

"*¡Salud!*" acknowledged Diego, clinking Brahim's glass.

After taking another thirst quenching gulp he said, "That was quite a night."

"It was, Diego! Thanks for helping. It seems you're a man of many talents too."

"My first profession was a barman."

"Well, you haven't forgotten how to be one."

"Hmm, guess not."

"I have had many jobs over the years, and I've always found each of them has continued to serve me in whatever I've chosen to do next."

"What other work have you done in the past?" asked Diego curiously.

"I've worked in the oil industry, engineering, and I've been an antique dealer. "

"You have an eye for old things, clearly," acknowledged Diego as he cast his eyes around the bar with its mosaic tiles and fine workmanship. "How long did it take to refurbish it?"

"Three years."

"Well, it's a wonderful achievement."

"You should have seen it before; it had been abandoned and was in a very poor state. My wife thought I was crazy to buy it."

"Your wife?"

"Yes, my wife. She didn't share my vision for the place and that was when we parted." Diego subsequently learned Brahim had been married twice before and had several grown-up children living in different parts of Europe.

Diego had already shared much of his story with Brahim, but hearing about Brahim's divorces, he felt obliged to tell him about his own recent divorce – explaining that the papers Brahim had posted on his behalf, were actually the signed divorce papers. Afterwards, Diego asked, "Where did your vision for this place come from... to open such a plush pilgrim *albergue*? It's like a palace."

"To serve. You see, I always believed I would gain more."

Diego ran a hand through his hair and eyed Brahim curiously. "What do you mean?"

"Growing up in the desert in Algeria I saw very clearly the struggles of life; none more so than in nature. But this struggle is necessary in order to experience the wonderful energy of life and its rewards. I have seen the pleasure of the falcon catching a mouse after hours scouring the landscape; caravans of thirsty camels drinking pleasurably at a remote waterhole, or foxes basking in the early morning sun after hunting all night. Myself, I would climb the dunes after completing my daily duties on our farm. I would watch the sun ebbing away on the horizon and experience the *sirocco* blowing across the sands.

"The more we become comfortable or pleasure seek, the less we appreciate these purifying moments of life. Travelling around France, Spain and Portugal selling my antiques, I witnessed the pilgrims on their walks, walking hard but experiencing such uplifting moments too. So when I saw an opportunity with this house near the route of the Camino, I felt compelled to buy it and contribute to the pilgrimage. Did you not hear pilgrims talking tonight about the sunrises or sunsets they've experienced, the wide horizons they've seen, birds gliding on the thermals or the meandering rivers they've walked beside? I could go on, but I think you understand what I'm saying?"

Diego nodded approvingly. "*Sí*, I heard them talk about these things tonight and I have experienced them myself. And you, which Camino have you walked?"

Brahim pulled himself up a stool and offered Diego a cigarette. After he'd taken one for himself, he replied, "I haven't walked one yet," then he winked, "but maybe that day will be sooner rather than later, if they reopen the bridge too soon."

"I hope you remain busy, but I can understand why

normally, pilgrims would want to end their day in Spain. Given it's so close."

Brahim puffed on his cigarette, his eyes softening with pleasure, before responding. "Today has shown me that pilgrims enjoy the hospitality of my house. So I am already halfway there to making it a success. Really, I am more than halfway there. Because here I am at the end of a busy day feeling like I'm sitting on top of a sand dune again."

"*Claro*, before, when I was a busker in Madrid's evening streets and put a finger to my strings, it felt as if I'd tamed a bull, watching the people in the city distracted by my music from their daily routines." He took a drag on his cigarette and eyed his beer. "Hmm, alcohol could never do that for me! Funny, I was even aware of it when my old maestro would push me hard in my guitar lessons and I'd sometimes catch him smiling."

"You get it. Music played well has the same power. It must be wonderful to be able to do that. I'd love to play an instrument at your level, Diego. Still, I play the drums and I find it fun."

"You keep surprising me. You play the drums too?"

"I try; there are a few musicians that live nearby and sometimes we meet, make a little party and play together. More than anything though I love flamenco; no other music is performed with as much passion and love. And the best are capable of producing *duende*."

Diego nodded with conviction, acknowledging the flamenco term, a word that was often mentioned by *flamencos* but was challenging to explain. Once he had even thought he was close to creating it, but he had confused it with *inori* and his friend, Daniel, all those years ago in Madrid had put him right on that. Diego sensed that Brahim felt *inori* too. He remembered how Daniel had explained that *inori* was a Japanese spiritual term, meaning self-belief and living a life without prejudice. Just as playing the guitar was like his prayer, his faith. But had he since evoked *duende*? Certainly, he never had when he had performed on those large stages under the scrutiny of Mark. He flicked the end of his cigarette into an ashtray, and then remarked, "Now I understand why you play Camarón de la Isla and Paco de Lucia."

"Exactly. The only modern flamenco artists who could consistently produce *duende*. Paco is irreplaceable, but Camarón de la Isla is my favourite. A singer is the heart and soul of flamenco and no one has ever sung as deeply as Camarón. He was a gypsy who gave everything."

"That's what some say, but others say he preferred alcohol and drugs."

They were interrupted by the tapping of a metal ring against iron followed by a soft voice in French asking, "*Bonsoir*, Brahim, you are still open?"

Diego cocked his head towards the window to see a bald man peering through its bars. Brahim nipped from behind the bar, opened the main door and ushered the man in. His name was Lucas and he introduced himself as an actor and musician. Immediately he recognised Diego.

"What are you doing here in Brahim's house?" Lucas said, switching to Spanish. "The rumour is that you have gone into rehab?"

Diego's jaw dropped. Then he laughed. "Well, I guess that's not far from the truth." He paused, looking for the words to explain his predicament, but Brahim found them for him.

"Diego is my friend and he is helping me while he recovers from a leg injury. He just needs a bit of rest and privacy." Brahim turned his gaze more directly towards Lucas and whispered, "And Lucas I know I can rely on you to keep this to ourselves?"

Lucas exchanged the look with a furrowed brow as he thought over Brahim's words. "Brahim you have so many interesting friends and I am honoured to meet another one of them." His voice deepened slightly as he continued, "This bar is my place of sanctuary too." Then he winked and said, "Anyway, if you let me drink for free tonight my lips are sealed."

Diego reached out an arm and shaking Lucas' hand said, "*Gracias* Lucas, I just need a little time to myself… that's all."

Brahim smiled cheerfully and served Lucas a glass of red wine. Pouring Diego and himself another small beer, Brahim again directed his gaze towards Lucas. "I intend to have an auction here, and that isn't a secret. Think you'd be able to help?"

Lucas rubbed his petite orange and brown goatee as his mind ticked over again. "Of course, when are you planning on holding it?"

"In three or four weeks. That will give me time to spread the word and get prepared."

"Perfect for me," replied Lucas turning his palms to the counter and tapping his fingers against the wood. "We should make it entertaining and give the guests another reason to spend their money on your antiques. Jazz would work well. You could play the drums?"

Brahim beamed. "That would be very nice."

Immediately Diego felt both sets of eyes on him. "*¡Qué va!*" he exclaimed, raising his hands in front of his chest. "I don't play jazz. Never have."

Lucas blinked but his eyes remained firmly on Diego. "Jazz is not what I'm best at either, but any opportunity to blow my sax is what I say."

"Hmm," muttered Diego, not quite knowing how to respond, but thinking there was some merit to Lucas' point. Musing further, he looked Lucas over. He was wearing a creased dark blazer and his trousers were equally rumpled. Aware of Diego looking at him, Lucas hooked a finger inside his mouth then yanked it out, producing a rhythmical popping sound. He repeated the exercise rapidly, simultaneously patting his other cheek with his palm, intimating percussion and rap, beatbox-style.

Diego laughed encouragingly and when Lucas was done with his impromptu performance, he leaned towards Diego and whispered. "I'm sure you'd play the guitar silky smooth, whether you're playing Miles Davis or Stravinsky."

Diego swilled the remains of his beer around his glass, before replying, "Lucas, you're very generous with your words, but I'm in rehab, remember?" He sank the dregs of beer and turned his gaze towards Brahim.

"I can pour you another," said Brahim, "but I will not join you. I must attend to the guests in the morning. Then I will take a drive to the beach and have my last bathe in the sea before it gets too cold."

Diego glanced at Lucas, but he was already standing up from his stool and attempting to pay for his wine, though Brahim crossed his arms refusing to accept his money. *Just a final beer*, Diego said inwardly, though something about the assertiveness of the men's actions and a sudden jarring confusion in his head suggested he'd be better off getting some fresh air and reflecting on things. He gently stretched himself off the stool, placing his feet with care on the floor, then he bid both men goodnight and left the bar and the house.

The moon was a pale sliver behind a patch of shifting cloud and barely lit the dim lane. Diego shifted his weight towards it but paused as the smell of cat's urine wafted his way. Feeling the hard cobbles through his shoes, his aching leg quivered as he remained facing the dark passage, continuing to think that the town centre offered the best option for a short stroll and a late drink. The mournful sound of *coo-cooo shooo* filled the air. Diego stiffened. Then silence. When again he heard the owl's wheezing cry he relaxed as the sound no longer felt eerie, more like a call to head towards it. The wind had carried the owl's nocturnal cooing from the river and Diego turned around, finding himself limping downhill. He passed through a medieval city gate and onto a trail of recently fallen leaves.

Diego soon arrived at the riverbank and paused to rest his leg. He looked out across the river, hoping to hear the owl again. But there were no sounds from the grove of ash trees, only his heavy breathing and the lapping of water. He cast a glance in the direction of the bridge. Its grey girders extended into the darkness. Then, the movement of shadowy figures sitting around a small fire, below on the riverbank, grabbed Diego's attention. Straining his ears, he overheard the deep voices of men, and a burst of hearty laughter coming from one of them. It sounded strangely familiar, yet Diego couldn't place it. *Possibly a walker I might have met?* he considered.

Curious to find out, he turned up his shirt collar and began hobbling towards the bridge. In the patches of moonlit river, he noticed the water bending around a small wooden quay. Getting closer Diego shuffled behind a tree to observe the scene further. The group were passing around a bottle of liquor and eating out of takeaway boxes. Most of them were sitting against hefty bags. He counted seven men in total and realised they were African street hawkers camping down for the night. The same deep, bellowing laugh came again, and in the light of the fire, Diego could see it was an older African man laughing, one whose stubble glinted silver. Immediately Diego felt he might find some affinity with the group of itinerants. He left the tree and hobbled over to them. Approaching, Diego could see that the laughing man was wearing a baseball cap with the letters 'USA' stitched into it.

The man looked up and nodded slightly. "Brother, you taking your time reaching Santiago." Then he looked down at Diego's feet and grinned. "Hope you're not looking to return the walking shoes."

"Man, don't worry, they've proven perfectly satisfactorily even though I haven't got very far. I had some setbacks, including breaking my pelvis."

"You alright now, brother?"

"Getting there, I think." Diego glanced at the bottle passing between hands and then at the man's feet and changed the subject. "And what about you, *amigo*? I don't see you wearing my old boots?"

"I save them for when I next go dancing in Mexico."

"Mexico?"

The man roared with laughter. "Mexico, Madrid or Santander. Wherever? I am hopeful *señoritas* will continue to enjoy dancing with this old man!"

Diego smiled fondly at him, but almost immediately the remark reminded him he'd never likely dance with Mari again, and his smile vanished. Solace was to be found in another drink and he eagerly accepted the bottle of aguardiente that was being offered around. He gingerly lowered himself down and propped his torso against one of the bags of merchandise. Sitting beside the older man, he shared his recent story with him but skimmed over the parts about his divorce, and the loss of his fortune. Exchanging names, Diego learned he was in the company of Wilfred. He and the other touts would be making their way up the Galician coast to work in the fish canneries.

The bottle was passed to Diego again. He took a drink from it, then another prolonged slug before handing it off to the man beside him. He leaned back further against the bag and looked about him. The clouds had passed the moon and he could now make out the twinkling of lights and the dark lines of trees on the opposite riverbank. In the air, he smelled the fresh, damp odour of pine. The trees ran neat and parallel with the ashes on his side of the bank and with the wind easing they were as still as the river. Yet, despite this, he sensed the river flowing, just as he sensed the warming aguardiente flowing through his arteries. His attention turned to some of the Africans. One added more sticks to the fire and poked it, so the flames flashed higher; a tall man stood beside the river, staring across it, while another with headphones, viewed flickering images on his phone.

Diego's attention shifted when Wilfred took out a harmonica from his shirt pocket, curled his large hands around it, and bringing the mouthpiece to his lips, bent his head to play. Diego had expected his melody to lament on the nostalgic but it was bright, and the bending high-pitched notes were lengthy and deliberate, each seeming to reach a place that offered hope in Diego's heart. He thought he heard the owl's hoots again mingling in between the harmonica's melody, but this time more distant. Diego rested his eyes, falling into that place halfway between wakefulness and sleep.

1 9

DAWN

Diego opened his eyes and caught the blurry images of migratory swifts darting across the river. Dawn was dissolving into a bright day and there was just a scattering of clouds in the sky. The fire had burnt itself out and Wilfred was brewing coffee on a camping stove. The only evidence there had been others there the night before were various indents in the grass. Diego had been sleeping on his back to protect his sore side and, sitting up, he pulled the woollen blanket he found covering his torso around his knees.

Hearing Diego rousing, Wilfred looked up. "Coffee your thing, brother?"

Croaky-throated, he answered, "*Absolutamente*. Nothing better than campfire coffee."

"Even better with a little aguardiente. Loosens the tonsils."

Diego wiped his eyes with his shirt cuff. "There's some left?"

"The boys left the remains."

"Wise move. It's strong stuff, reckon it knocked me out."

"It's a man's drink, for sure, but you needed the rest."

"Did you throw the blanket over me?"

"It was one of the younger brothers. From his stock."

Diego half-smiled. Wilfred glanced round at the coffee pot hissing and rose to his feet. Diego observed the coffee simmering its oily liquid around the pot's silver spout, thinking it was a drink to take neat and in the open. So, when Wilfred poured him some into a cup, he passed on adding the aguardiente to it.

Diego sipped his coffee, and then asked, "Why didn't you leave with the others?"

Wilfred sat back, poured himself some coffee, and then replied, "'cause I'm told there are opportunities in this town."

"Who spun you that line?"

Wilfred casually gestured at the river with his mug and replied, "It."

Diego glanced at the Miño, thinking he'd misunderstood, and that Wilfred was likely referring to something else, but all he could see ahead of them was the river. "You mean the river?"

"Yes, *señor*," replied Wilfred, his look unfamiliarly serious. "Nature is full of messages. We are also part of nature. And you brought me a message too, Diego. You've shown me this old man needs to give his big feet a rest."

"I have?"

"You were walking in my shoes and look what happened to you. That's the message you brought me. Time for me to slow down, before I take a big fall too. Not so easy to recover when you have older bones." Wilfred tilted his head up towards the bridge. "Listen… Tell me what you hear?"

"Not much?"

"Exactly, Diego. No vehicles, no people overhead. Repairs could last a long time."

"Perhaps? So what?" Diego said doubtfully, beginning to think that Wilfred might be a little *loco*. Sarcastically, he added, "Did the river tell you when the bridge would reopen?"

Wilfred sighed slightly and set his cup down in the grass. "You mock me, brother?"

Diego sensed disappointment in Wilfred's eyes and felt slightly ashamed. Not only had he been disrespectful to an elder, but in that moment, he recalled the words of another ageing man, who had said that there was knowledge to be found in water's depths. Remigio, the wise old man he'd encountered in the fishing village near Porto, had impressed upon him that the waterways could teach him something about the 'truth'. How curious he had been to discover more about this mysterious belief. How accepting he once was to the magic of things along the roads of his previous Caminos. Yet, how easily he was now prepared to dismiss alternative beliefs, just because they didn't sit easily in his mind. *Have I become that bitter?* he thought. This astute, gentle man he was now in the company of wasn't *loco*; he himself was the crazy one. How could he have written off Wilfred so casually?

Diego unwrapped the blanket from around his knees and slowly raised himself off the ground. He stood with legs slightly astride and breathed in the chill of the new day. Then he threw the dregs of his coffee into the ashes from the fire and reached a hand down to Wilfred. The African smiled and took hold of Diego's hand. Wilfred's grip was strong and as Diego helped him to his feet, he sensed in him the weighty bones of a well-travelled man. "I think it's going to be a beautiful day," whispered Diego.

"Always," answered Wilfred nodding. "But this morning it will rain."

Diego looked up at the bluish sky and ribbons of clouds, squinting as his eyes adjusted to the brightening light. "Really? What makes you say that – the river told you?"

Wilfred exploded with laughter. "I don't always need its

help; some things this old man can work out for himself. In my work, you quickly learn when the weather will help with the selling of certain products. You feel the cool breeze this morning?"

"Go on?"

"It's the autumn wind and will bring rain from the Atlantic."

"It will?"

"Often," replied Wilfred glancing northwestward and nodding at the hills across the river. "Reason they call that part Green Spain."

Diego looked up, now noticing the distant dark clouds. "Hmm, I must have missed those before."

"Experience," replied Wilfred matter-of-factly. "Now, I need to buy a boat."

"What! You're joking, right? Thought you were going to say umbrellas."

Wilfred grinned, managing to control any further outbursts of laughter.

"Normally, yes. Though remember, brother, I got to find a living where I can take the weight off my feet. The detour to the other bridge adds a couple of kilometres to the pilgrims' walk, but the direct route is across the water. Better for pilgrims, and also good for a man with a ferry. Don't you think?"

Diego stretched his eyes across the wide river. "What kind of boat were you thinking of?"

"Small boat. Will you help me?"

Diego's attention briefly turned upwards to the incoming clouds before he looked back around to face Wilfred. "Can you even swim?" Wilfred shook his head. "Well, hell, if you can't swim what have I got to worry about. Okay, Wilfred, I'll help you until my leg fully recovers, or they reopen the bridge. Whichever comes first."

Wilfred nodded, his resolute mind already working on his

idea. Then they heard the light patter of rain on the river, like the first tentative steps of a *bailaora*, flamenco dancer, finding her rhythm. Diego glanced at the raindrops causing ripples in the river. Then he hurried as best he could to help Wilfred gather his packs before the downpour came.

NAVIGATING THE RIVER

A month had passed since Wilfred had purchased the little boat. He hadn't haggled with the man at the rowing club; he thought the price he asked was fair. He took it as a sign of good fortune that the club was selling off its old boats. It was a traditional rowboat made of wood, rowed by one person from the rear seat, and could carry three passengers in front, plus their backpacks. A lick of red paint was all it had taken to make it shine again. Wilfred had put up a notice in Brahim's guesthouse – where he was now also staying – promoting his ferry service, and it brought enough pilgrims to make several daily crossings of the river.

Diego's body was healing fast, and he was happy doing most of the rowing, leaving Wilfred attending to those customers who came down to the quay. It gave him reason to get out from under Brahim's feet now that his guesthouse was busy. He had also enjoyed the challenge of navigating the boat across the river, determining how to row transversely upstream and not directly against the currents. So the river's ripples then guided the little vessel downstream, and neatly across to the opposite quay. He taught Wilfred how to feather the oars, rotating them sideways after each stroke and how to turn by rowing with just one firm arm. Though his friend had comfortably grasped the technique, he readily passed back the oars to Diego. They also adapted their crossing times to work with the tides.

Diego had almost sailed away from his old life. The Spanish tax authorities were now off his back following the express sale of his penthouse and other assets; the little left-over had gone to Mari. The only connection to his past were his occasional thoughts of what Mari might be doing at that moment. But things were definitely simpler: his share of the ferry takings and occasional shifts at the bar covered his room expenses, and Brahim always made sure Diego ate well and didn't go thirsty. Diego was satisfied in thinking of Santiago as somewhere on a distant horizon; it felt enough just to briefly catch the stories of the pilgrims he gave passage to. He'd also let his beard grow and now no one ever recognised him. Being out of the limelight had something to do with that too.

His leg was almost better and it dawned on him that he would soon have to leave Wilfred and the boat. Evidently, the pressure Diego was putting against his limb as he stretched it out and rowed was helping it heal quickly. So, one slow afternoon as they waited by the quay for passengers, Diego asked Wilfred when he was thinking of taking over from him. After all, it was his boat, and splitting the takings wasn't sustainable.

Wilfred glanced at the boat bobbing up and down beside the quay and said warmly, "Whenever you're ready, brother."

"Whenever I'm ready?"

"I will take you across the river."

"What makes you think I want to cross the river?"

"You will want to return home." Diego shook his head doubtfully. Wilfred's reaction was to tether the boat for the night and invite Diego for a drink.

They arrived at Brahim's bar and took their drinks in the

courtyard, sitting at a table where the sun leaned in. Brahim served them beers and olives and then went about his business.

After chewing on an olive Wilfred casually asked Diego, "Have you learned anything from the river?"

Diego removed his Stetson and shifted his torso towards the autumn rays. He took a sip of beer. After a long pause, he said, "We can't control it, but we can navigate it if we learn its ways." He put his glass down and thought over his observation; not completely sure of the words that had just come out of his mouth. The river hadn't spoken directly to him like Wilfred had insinuated it did to him, neither had it revealed some deep knowledge or 'truth', as Remigio had put it. All he knew was what he sensed in the oars when he dipped them into the water, and how the little vessel would rock when he pushed it too hard against the currents. Most of what he heard whilst rowing had been like static noise through a speaker, the wind through the treetops, and the sloshing of water against the boat. Nonetheless, he trusted Wilfred's intuition and it felt like the moment to fully confide in him. Thus, Diego told Wilfred about wrecking his marriage and his fears about starting all over again. He also mentioned his growing doubts about walking away from his rock career.

Wilfred listened intently and when Diego was done talking he said, "But you're still here."

"*Sí*, but…"

"…Life is the only stage, brother," interjected Wilfred. "I once lived on small farm in Ghana with my wife and son. My wife would sell our produce at a market in Accra and one day she brought my boy to the market to help. He was only five years old, but already very independent. On that day he saw cars stopped at traffic lights and he ran up to them to sell leftover papaya slices. But is very dangerous when the cars move again, and he chased after a man in a car who expressed interest in the papaya. But my son didn't watch the road for cars coming another way, and a car hit him. He was instantly killed. After that, my wife got very depressed, and then one day she drowned herself in the sea."

Diego offered Wilfred a sympathetic smile. He cupped his hands together and lowered his head, closing his eyes. His attention was drawn fully into Wilfred's story and he saw himself in Africa and observing the dark soil of the farm. The gurgles from the fountain providing the faintest reminder they remained in the courtyard and not in Africa. "I couldn't face losing the farm too. It was the only memory I had left of them, so I tried to work the farm and market stall on my own. But it was very difficult without my wife. Then came the drought, and my crops began to die. Soon the animals got hungry and monkeys moved in on what fruit I had left in the trees. Monkeys are very fast and they kept me running after them all day. But one day a neighbour showed me how to make traps for them with coconuts." Wilfred explained that he learned to hollow out coconuts at one end and tie them to his trees. The hole was just wide enough to slide a monkey's hand through it, as well as a banana, which he placed inside each coconut as bait. A troublesome monkey would discover a banana inside the coconut and grab at it through the hole, gripping it with a tight fist, and in the process trapping itself.

"Monkeys just stay there, stuck, gripping the banana. All they have to do is let go to be free. But not one monkey ever did that and I always captured them in this trap." Wilfred let out one of his booming three-beat laughs. "Humans are like monkeys."

Diego unwrapped his hands and raised his head to look at Wilfred. The fountain reflected in his eyes and he discovered himself part completing the story. "But you were different, weren't you Wilfred. That's when you freed yourself?"

Wilfred's laughter lines relaxed, the folds across his forehead softened and he smiled benevolently at Diego. "Eventually," he paused, "one morning, in the silence of dawn when I went to the traps and saw another tired monkey, very pale, I grasped I was that monkey and stuck in my past. That day I handed back to my landlord the keys of the farm and I went to Accra. I began mourning the loss of my family, but there I also learned how to sell anything in the streets. Shortly after, I discovered how to make my way to Europe."

After Wilfred was done telling his story they drank in silence. Several minutes passed. Diego wasn't sure what to say next. Wilfred's story was as unjust as the most sorrowful of Camarón de la Isla's songs, yet its sentiment was as convincing as many other gypsy inspired rhythms too. Those songs captured the restless essence of living in the moment. And though the sentiments of Wilfred's story echoed his present situation he still wasn't ready to address his mental barrier.

Wilfred's mind had turned to his immediate future. It was the first time since leaving the farm he had felt settled in a place. He believed pilgrims would still continue to use his ferry service after the work on the bridge was completed. At the same time, he wasn't ignorant to the fact that at some point, the city authorities would come and close down his unofficial business. But Wilfred's thoughts remained unruffled. He had learned years ago that as long as he remained alert to opportunities, problems had a way of figuring themselves out.

More pilgrims arrived after their days' walking, and although Brahim remained calm as his house began to fill, Diego could see him dashing between the bar, kitchen and bedrooms. "I must go and help Brahim in the bar." He stood up to leave and with a thoughtful smile said, *"Gracias."* Wilfred lifted his right hand and dipped the peak of his cap at Diego in silent acknowledgement.

The bar kept Diego busy that night, but when he was able to take a quick break and step outside for a smoke, his eyes were immediately drawn back inside. From the doorway he observed two middle-aged women jigging to the world beats from the sound system; new companions huddled in one corner, grinning mischievously at their inside jokes from the day, as they found another reason to raise their glasses and knock their drinks back. Beyond them, in the dining area, he glimpsed a party around a table, eating well, reminding Diego how good food could taste after a hard day's walking. He also saw a couple taking a closer look at a large Moroccan floor lamp, which he hadn't previously noticed. Then he spotted more antiques dotted around the bar area, including a large clay pot and a lute. Attached to the antiques were price tags. Brahim was testing the market.

Diego stubbed out his cigarette on a cobble and looking back up he felt he was witnessing a gathering that shared a secret: a celebratory communion with the power to lift up the soul. They were pilgrims on the Camino from several countries, yet they could just as easily be an indigenous tribe celebrating an ancient rite. It crossed his mind that this unfathomable energy he was witnessing took several other forms; something that the modern world was losing touch with. *Is duende the same?* Again, Diego pondered if he'd ever got close to producing it, but his thoughts were immediately diverted by a crowd building at the bar, and he darted back inside.

He worked well behind the bar, with the rapid precision and rhythm of a *flamenco*. No one's glass stayed empty long and all were delighted by his native flair. Later, with the drinkers' lust for alcohol satisfied and the bar cleared, one of the middle-aged women whom he'd glimpsed earlier when smoking outside stepped over to the bar, and leaning into it, looked to catch Diego's eye.

She coughed and ran a hand through her long brown hair, which was accentuated with burgundy colouring. "Hey *guapo*, looks like you need a drink?"

Diego looked up from the glasses he was drying with a

bar towel, drawn in by her directness. She had called him handsome in Spanish, with a Catalan accent. He gazed at her playful eyes and replied, "Are you from Barcelona?"

"How did you know?"

"I'm very good with accents," he replied as he found his mind persuading him that this new life he found himself in wasn't a bad way to live. There would always be women passing through here and he would never really need to explain himself to them.

"So, who am I buying a drink for?" the woman said fluttering her long eyelashes.

Almost impulsively, Diego shifted his expression into a wide grin, his face aching as he did so as if his facial muscles were no longer supportive of his fake rock star smile. Just as he was about to give her his name, he relaxed the corners of his mouth, thinking this was a futile game he was about to play. He might be able to have sex with this *señora*, but it wouldn't be anything else. Moreover, as with all the flings he'd had before meeting Mari, all he'd been doing again was jumping into the dark eddies of his river. So Diego found himself saying, "*Gracias*, but I'm good."

The woman blushed slightly, noting the firmness in his response. She responded by taking a final sip from her beer bottle and setting it down hard on the counter, and hissing, "*¡Buenos noches!*"

De nada, you're welcome, Diego sarcastically thought. She was not a patch on Mari.

When Brahim decided to close for the night, remaining in the bar were Diego, Lucas and Wilfred, who had joined them for a nightcap. They sat on stools around the curved end of the counter, and when Brahim had given everyone a drink, he announced, "I feel ready to hire some staff."

Diego thought for a moment, wondering if it was worth discouraging Brahim's aspirations, still convinced that as soon as the bridge reopened he would be back to square one.

Though it didn't make sense to take the shine off the evening, and since Wilfred remained confident in his ferry service, he bit his tongue. He did, however, raise an eyebrow at Lucas, whose reaction was barely indifferent.

Brahim then stepped back to the till area and from a drawer reached for a stack of leaflets. Placing them on the bar he asked everyone, "What do you think of these?"

Wilfred picked one up and eyeing the leaflet closely said, "Very nice, print some extra and I will share with my shop friends."

Diego glanced at Wilfred. "You've made friends with the storekeepers?"

"I also put leaflets in the shops advertising the ferry service."

Brahim smiled. "Very good – I will get some more printed tomorrow."

Suddenly reminded of the auction and its festivities, Diego enquired as casually as he could, "It's going ahead, then?"

"Very much so," replied Brahim. He glanced towards Lucas. "This Saturday, with jazz too – everything is ready. Lucas?"

Lucas turned to Diego, replying, "Mostly."

"This coming Saturday?" muttered Diego.

"Yes, at the end of the week," confirmed Brahim.

Lucas remained looking at Diego, but now with an expectant expression across his face. Diego turned away from his gaze and looked towards Brahim. "I can help with the bar, no problem. But as I mentioned before, I've never played jazz."

"Thank you, Diego, your help behind the bar is always appreciated," said Brahim as he went over to a table to collect some empty glasses.

"Goodnight gentlemen," said Wilfred standing up from his stool and placing his empty glass down.

A mountain of excuses ran through Diego's head now he

was on his own with Lucas. However, Lucas got in there first, his voice finding a deeper tone as he stated, "Paco de Lucia took to jazz like a duck to water. Man, he was a fucking swan!"

Diego uttered meekly, "But I'm no Paco de Lucia." Lucas' eyes narrowed as he scrutinised Diego, and a few moments passed without a word until Diego yielded and said, "You're deluded if you think I was ever in his league. Besides, I'm done with music."

Lucas pushed his shoulders back and sat up straight on his stool. "No sane swan would clip its own wings. And it would be remiss of me not to take the opportunity to perform with a guitar legend like yourself."

Finally, Diego understood. Performing at the auction had nothing to do with his insecurities – it was about inspiring Lucas to reach higher and perhaps inspire others. Yet, still, he felt anxious: not only had he not lifted a guitar in many weeks, he would also have to adapt to jazz. Submitting, Diego nodded at Lucas and said, "You do know I'm broke?"

Lucas' eyes radiated with enthusiasm. "Don't you worry about that, Diego – we'll find you a flamenco guitar by Saturday." Then he jumped down from his stool and gestured with some money at Brahim, who was now loading the dishwasher. Again, Brahim shook his head kindly, refusing his payment, and with a broad smile, Lucas left the bar.

Diego remained sitting at the bar as Brahim finished up the last tasks for the night. On impulse, he grabbed the laptop from behind the counter and logged onto his Facebook fan page. The interaction with his fans had all but dried up. Diego wasn't surprised. Then, even though he knew it was probably a bad idea, he clicked on Mari's Facebook profile. It *was* a bad idea! Immediately he spied several images of her cuddling up to another man. Worse, it was a man he knew – Carlos Pepi, his support act from the aborted concert. "*¡Qué*

Cabrón!" exclaimed Diego in disbelief, as he slammed down the screen of the computer.

Brahim popped his head through the kitchen doorway. "Everything is okay Diego?"

"*Sí,*" murmured Diego. But it wasn't. He might almost have tolerated Mari meeting someone so soon if it had been a man her own age, and a stranger. But this was too much. He felt like he'd been kicked in the gut. Carlos Pepi was almost old enough to be her father, and it begged further questions. Had they been at it for a while, since even before their breakup? Was it about money and security? But he didn't know those answers. He stared vacantly through the window into the dark alleyway, wishing that he had died that night he had fallen from the balcony, feeling he really was at the end of his road. After a while, he got up from the stool, sighed deeply and poured himself a whisky.

DIFFERENT PATHS

The rest of the week passed in a fog of indecision as Diego rowed back and forth between Spain and Portugal, grumpy and clenching at the oars. If he'd been asked to recall the weather, the nature of the river, or the conversations he'd had, he wouldn't have been able to. His mind had become overwhelmed with figuring out his next move. Several times he had attempted to write a pros and cons list in his head of the merits of leaving Valença. But every time he tried, he'd lose control of the oars and come close to rolling the boat. Diego had only become aware that it was the end of the week when they were securing the boat one evening and Wilfred mentioned it was the day of the auction.

Diego's irresolute mind tethered him to the spot and he told Wilfred to go on, that he would join him later after a smoke. Wilfred nodded politely in reply and set off for the guesthouse. Diego looked out across the river; it was dark and offered nothing. Then he remembered he'd stashed his hipflask in the boat and reached down to grab it from under the seat. He pulled off the stopper and winced as he took a sip from it. It burned the back of his throat and tasted of paint stripper. He set the flask down on the riverbank and went about rolling himself a cigarette.

A chalky half-moon was now visible above the westerly hills, and behind him, crows were taking their places in the trees for the night. Diego was virtually motionless, his smoking nostrils the only sign of his consciousness. Suddenly the crows cawed menacingly and Diego shivered, sensing their goading. He flicked his cigarette into the river and spun around, looking upwards at the trees. Clapping and flailing his arms furiously, he bellowed, "You scavengers, don't fuck with me too!" As the startled birds flew away Diego continued, "If only you knew what it felt like to have your eyes pecked out... and be left with nothing!" He turned and his eyes followed the black birds across the grey-blue sky before they settled into a holm oak further upstream. He returned his attention to the river and regarded the water, his words becoming more emotional, rambling then wailing, as if he was begging the river to listen and give him something, "...I pimped my music until it sounded like the Gipsy Kings on acid. But we lived well because of that; Mari never had to worry about anything anymore. But still, she left me *¡Puta Madre!* That bitch has destroyed me."

Diego paused and took a breath. He didn't know what to do next. There was nothing else he could do, other than continue securing the boat. He trudged over to it and began hauling it further ashore. Arriving at the boat's resting place on the bank, he saw something bright in the gravel. He leaned down to see what it was. It was the skeletal thighbone of a goat. He picked it up to take a closer look – the crows and Iberian sun had cleaned and bleached it to stunning whiteness. He took hold of the bone just below the swell of the joint with his left hand and, cupping the other end in his right to steady it, fretted out a mute and manic gypsy lament. As his left hand ran up and down the length of the bone he rocked his arms and shoulders to the rhythm of the music that only he could hear. He was crying and his mouth gaped and twisted in pain. Then, suddenly, he dropped to his knees, leaned back and hammered out a trembling note of sustained and utter silence.

The crows watched Diego from their roost in the old oak. Their cold black eyes met his dark eyes. Diego knew what they wanted him to do. His hand tightened on the bone shank until he held it as cruelly as he had held the neck of his guitar just before he had smashed it to pieces on the stage in Porto. He raised the bone above his head and brought it down over and over again onto the soft brow of the bank, pounding the turf to pulp. But unlike his guitar, the bone stayed true and did not break. Eventually, Diego tired and dropped the bone. He was panting, but motionless, like a seabird on a rock figuring out its next move. Finally, he got to his feet and went over to the river's edge. He looked down into its dark watery mass and whispered, "We were always on different paths."

He crouched down and cupped a hand into the water to wash away his tears. Bending his head closer to the river he placed his other hand on the crown of his Stetson to stop it from falling in. Briefly, he caught sight of his shadowy reflection across the strip of moonlit river before a cloud passed across the moon and it was lost. What he had seen was a muscular strumming arm bent at the elbow, supporting a hat with a wide-angled brim, snuggly fitting its wearer. And the head that appeared from underneath the hat was shaped like a curved half-moon, with eyes as deep as craters. In the calm river, he'd just seen the kernel of the man he'd never given a proper chance to be: Diego – the flamenco guitarist. Diego stretched his arm out towards where he'd earlier put down his whisky flask and grabbed hold of it. Then he stood up and threw the flask into the river. It received his offering in silence. Next, he turned to face the crows and bowed to them.

He started in the direction of Brahim's house and as his pace quickened, he realised he was no longer dragging his left leg. Striding up the hill, his mind turned to the gig and he wondered what type of guitar Lucas might have laid his hands on. From down the street, Diego could hear, "…fifty euros, is that all? 150, thank you, 200…" It was Brahim's voice, rich in tone and theatrical, and Diego immediately sensed his house was humming with people.

The main door of the bar was wide open and Diego squeezed his way in through the crowd. He noticed two new faces working behind the bar – a youthful couple, exchanging furtive glances with each other between their tasks. He continued through to the courtyard and saw that small Moroccan lanterns had been placed on each table. At them sat well-dressed guests, the shadows of their upper limbs waving frantically across the walls as they competed with each other in the game of bidding. A middle-aged, lean and willowy man, was stealthily topping up their champagne glasses. Against the far wall was a stage lit by spotlights, where Brahim was standing behind an oak lectern with a micro-phone in hand. Close to the stage and scribbling into a notepad was Wilfred. Brahim brought his gavel down hard onto the lectern, and a thickset man jumped up from his table and punched the air.

Brahim proclaimed, "Sold to the *senhor* at the far table, and may I say you would make an excellent dealer, you got this ancient urn for a very good price." Standing on tiptoe, Diego noticed the clay pot from the bar had been placed in front of the stage. Lucas was with a short man dressed in a black suit and had the look of a musician. They collected the pot between them and then disappeared into an adjoining room. When they returned, they were carrying a vintage rocking horse.

Brahim stepped down from the stage. Playfully he announced, "Which *Senhora*, would like to take this antique rocking horse home to their children? It was once ridden by the happy children of a sultan." The eyes of the bidders gleamed and Brahim was soon leading a woman in a blue dress to the horse and helping her sit astride it. He began the bidding as she merrily rocked up and down, and the price of the horse was soon bid up. Diego watched on from the rear of the courtyard as Brahim steered the proceedings like the master conductor of an orchestra, and many artefacts from his cellar rapidly passed through the auction. Brahim created a story around each item, and they all sold for hefty prices.

With the auction winding down, Diego felt his shoulders pinch and tighten as he thought about the imminent concert. However, throughout the frenetic auction, Brahim had remained self-assured and steady, reminding Diego of his papá's calm nature at the candyfloss cart. And this brought to mind his father's words of advice. Inwardly he repeated them, *Take a deep breath, draw the guitar in close and think about how you feel today.*

Lucas brought out the last piece, and instantly Diego fell under its spell. It was a Spanish guitar, and as Diego craned his neck to get a better look at it, he could tell it was made with a flamenco artist in mind. Maybe a guitar he'd played before, perhaps many times? It resembled his papá's old guitar. "*Loco?*" Diego whispered. Knowing it was madness to consider that notion, given how long ago he'd returned a similar-looking guitar to its rightful owner: Papá's apparition. Nonetheless, the fading sheen and wear along its neck looked distinctly familiar. Diego could only guess at how it might have ended up in Brahim's basement.

From the stage, Brahim caught Diego's eye and he smiled at him. "Today, amongst us is a flamenco genius, and he will be performing with this guitar in the concert following the auction," said Brahim, generating curiosity amongst the guests. Lucas passed Brahim the guitar and holding it up so everyone could see it better, he declared, "It's a classic." He plucked a string, and as its tone reverberated around the courtyard the candle flames quivered inside the lamps, casting shadows as if they were flamenco *bailors* limbering up to dance.

The moment reminded Diego of the time he'd taken Papá's guitar to a luthier's workshop to be repaired, during his first Camino, and testing a string it also had made the shadows tremor. Now practically convinced of its former ownership Diego couldn't risk losing it; he'd have to bid for it though the last time he'd checked, he had not much more than a hundred euros to his name.

Brahim continued, "So, who will start the bidding with fifty euros for this incredible guitar?" Almost immediately a sharp-faced elderly man, wearing square glasses and a wool blazer subtly nodded his head. However, the brim of the flat cap he was wearing exaggerated his nod and it didn't go unnoticed by Brahim, nor by Diego.

Another person in the room bid before the elderly man wearing the flat cap nodded briefly again, taking the price up to €100. Diego grimaced, not quite knowing what to do, thinking that not so long ago he could have written a blank cheque to get hold of it. There was nothing else he could do but bid. Diego raised his arm high, cleared his throat and called out, "One hundred and one euros and every last cent I have."

Brahim responded, "Very good, Diego, we now have confirmation of the guitar's potential."

The elderly man raised his bid to €300. Brahim smiled sympathetically at Diego before his attention was drawn back to the action and the brewing bidding war. From the side of the stage, Lucas had just bid €400, and in response to the elderly man's counter bid of €500, Wilfred raised his fist, glanced at Diego, then at the elderly man, and assertively declared, "We settle this now – one thousand euros."

Diego circled his way round to the stage and with a shrug of his shoulders, a gesture of his palms and a wild shake of his head he cautioned Wilfred to act rationally and think of himself. However, Wilfred did not renounce his offer, and all eyes in the courtyard turned to the elderly man. The man removed his glasses and began wiping them with a handker-chief, and although he was squinting, the packed courtyard sensed his mind ticking over. With his lenses polished he returned his spectacles to his face; they rode high on his prominent nose. Then he said coolly, "Two thousand euros."

A hush filled the space and everyone fixated on Wilfred, including Brahim, but reluctantly Wilfred shook his head. Brahim gave the room a few moments before he struck his gavel onto the lectern. The wood creaked, as did Diego's bones. Brahim congratulated the elderly man, before reminding him and the audience that the auction of the guitar had been subject to it first being played in the forthcoming concert. The man responded by tipping his cap.

Diego patted Wilfred on the shoulder and asked, "What made you do that?"

Without a suggestion of a smile or his usual booming laughter, Wilfred replied, "'Cause you're now ready to cross the river."

Diego's eyes slanted. "How do you know that?"

"For the first time, I sense you truly wanted something."

"You did?"

"As if that guitar was a part of you."

Two tall men then joined them. The taller of them was wearing an office suit that matched his dark features and dangling around his neck was a chain of civic office. The shorter man shook Wilfred's hand and introduced him to his taller associate, the city mayor.

The movement of activity on the stage and the arrival of Lucas with the guitar in one hand and his saxophone in another, diverted Diego's attention. Diego turned to face the stage and saw it had already been organised for the jazz concert: somehow a drum set, synthesiser and music stands had been packed onto the little stage.

"You ready?" said Lucas facing the stage too and passing Diego the guitar.

Diego nodded. "So Lucas, you didn't have to look very far to find me a guitar, then?"

Lucas tilted his head in the direction of the adjoining room and basement. "It's an Aladdin's cave in there."

Brahim arrived on the stage and Lucas urged Diego to take his place and introduced him to his companion in the black suit, the pianist. Sitting on a chair, Diego crossed one leg over the other, and then positioned the curve of the guitar's body on his thigh. It wasn't the lightest of flamenco guitars, but he sensed its dependability. He ran his fretting hand along its neck and slid his playing hand down its spruce top. Instinctively he found its dimples and abrasions. Diego smiled and expectantly turned his attention to the sound hole. He eyed the words of *La guitarra del Peregrino*, The Pilgrim's guitar, etched into the rosette. There it was, confirmation that he had been reunited with his own guitar, not Papá's old one. It was the guitar Diego had bought himself upon arriving in Santiago.

Brother, we'd better make the most of this, Diego said silently, aware he would have to hand the guitar over to its new owner after the show. He reached for the pegs and set about tuning the instrument, but to his surprise, the strings hadn't slackened off, and each note sparkled as if they'd been played only yesterday. The courtyard lights were dimmed further, and the spotlights fell upon Diego. He glanced over his right shoulder to see Lucas, who winked back at him, as he readied himself with his saxophone. Over his right shoulder was Brahim, sitting patiently at the drum kit, as if he'd been there all evening, and to his right was the pianist, hands poised over his synthesiser.

Diego bent his head towards the guitar, drawing in a long breath. Then he closed his eyes and the audience fell silent. He sensed the soft pitter-patter skips of the fountain and stiffened a finger across a fret. His playing hand brushed the strings across the body of the guitar. The notes rolled easily together, yet each stroke was crisp, as were the tones that came from the taps at its body. In his low notes, Diego sensed the depths of rivers, and in his highest ones were the mists that spread through the valleys.

After some rapid fingerpicking, Diego brought the sequence to an abrupt close. Lucas took up the reigns, putting his lips to his saxophone, and the other musicians accompanied him and the performance resumed its journey. Though the jazz musicians sometimes referred to their music sheets, Diego was able to anticipate their notes and follow them. But always the musicians would suddenly make way for Diego and his acoustic solos. In his hands, the guitar was rapid, smooth; violent, faint-hearted. The instrument had become an extension of himself and was connecting to the same mysterious source as that within the cascading fountain.

Then, amidst another solo, as his flexing fingers flowed like liquid, he became conscious of the lyrics of one of Camarón de Isla's most famous songs: *Como el agua*, To be like water. From somewhere inside, he perceived Camarón's primordially hoarse voice – his lengthened tones a force of nature, with the power to penetrate the darkness and heal within. In that song, he'd sung of clear water running down from the mountains and his body walking cheerfully. And in that moment of revelation, Diego understood just like water, for love to become pure, it must endure the journey and return to its source. Despite Camarón's addictions and problems, he must have known that once everything was stripped back, love remained.

Diego opened his eyes and saw that several members of the audience were leaning back contently in their seats with their eyes closed, whilst a few others were sitting with bowed, calmed heads. He glanced around at Lucas and Brahim, and they smiled back at him. Diego turned his head back to the audience; no longer was there any hint of the boisterous behaviour that had consumed them during the auction. Diego shivered as he considered whether he had just touched them with some kind of *duende*? Seeing the crowds go ecstatic in the large concert halls had never felt as good as this.

LIFE'S RIVER

Diego stuffed the football shirt and the extra items of clothing he'd bought during his stay in Valença into his backpack and fastened it. Then he propped it against the wall as he stepped out onto the balcony. The morning sky was pebble-blue, pitted with the odd cloud, and the sun had just climbed above the forested hills, drying the land from a rain shower during the night. He gazed out across the river and breathed in the morning air, noting an infusion of damp vines, roses and mossy fields. Swifts flew in wide circles, their shrilling sounds announcing it was a good day for travelling.

Raising a palm to his cleanly shaved face, Diego thought over Wilfred's remark of a week ago: "You will want to return home." Now he understood what he'd meant by that. Crossing the Miño River into Spain was about coming home to himself. It felt so obvious now. He was still on the Camino, though he had meandered some, much like the river itself does on its way to the ocean. He was coming full circle and returning to Santiago. Practically circumnavigating Spain. So much had happened during those last nine or so years. Returning from the Mediterranean coast, he'd forged self-belief, sealed with gumption, only to betray love for his demons and a place in celebrity society. However, he felt redemption was close.

A knock at the door distracted his thoughts. He left the balcony and opened the door. Braham was standing there holding up his guitar.

"But I handed it to the *señor* after the show?"

"You did, Diego," said Brahim with a childlike grin.

"So he's returned it?"

Brahim stepped into the room and glanced at Diego's backpack against the wall before he held out the guitar. "In a way. I just bought it back from him."

"*¡Madre mia!*" said Diego taking the guitar and cradling it in his arms. "*¿Por qué?* I don't understand – he seemed desperate to have it?"

"He had his reasons, but I am no worse off, as I bought it back with his cash, and this is now my gift to you."

"But that's a lot of money to forgo. Plus, you'll need it... to help you through when the bridge reopens."

"Diego, Diego – I might easily have gone under if you hadn't helped me when I couldn't afford staff. You got me to this stage, and now I am set."

"You're set?"

Brahim explained that following the concert he'd had a late drink with the city's new mayor and the head of the local Rotary Club. Wilfred had met the Rotary Club man through his storekeeper friends and made the introductions. The long and short of it was that the mayor wanted to put Valença back on the tourist map and compete directly with Tui for pilgrim business. He believed that one of the first ways to do that was to promote Brahim's guesthouse as the last pilgrim hostel in Portugal. Signage directing pilgrims off the Camino to the house would be erected, aided by a tourism campaign promoting the city's medieval history.

Furthermore, learning about Wilfred's little ferry service had given the mayor another idea. Originally, before the bridge, a ferry service had operated between the two border towns. The mayor's idea was to officially revive the service. And the town hall would subsidise Wilfred in buying a larger ferry to provide it. Moreover, some historians believed St. James had first arrived in the Iberian Peninsula via the Miño estuary, and the mayor would see to it that his tourism department wouldn't lose a trick in promoting the ferry service as pivotal in the Santiago story.

"So was the *señor* who bid for the guitar a member of the Rotary or a friend of the mayor?" asked Diego.

"Perhaps. He's a collector and has a kind of antique store in town. There are all sorts of things there, from vintage radios to French tables." Brahim smiled. "I think I might be able to do some future business with him."

"Hmm, but did he need much persuading to sell back the guitar?"

"You want the truth, Diego?"

"Go on," replied Diego undeterred.

"Well, he took a closer look at the guitar and thought it was overrated. He also looked at your rock profile. It's not highly ranked anymore, it seems. Guess I sold you too well in the auction, Diego."

Diego smiled. "Just shows it's not only teenagers who rate stardom over substance." He tapped the side of the guitar. "But this old *amigo* doesn't care what others think."

"Very much so, Diego. A painter must paint what is in their heart, as must a musician play what's in theirs."

Diego went to place the guitar by his pack, but he stopped midway and turning back round to face Brahim asked, "Where did you find the guitar?"

Brahim thought for a moment and then his eyes began to shine when he remembered. "I found it in a flea market in Madrid… when I was on the road as an antique dealer."

Diego's eyes narrowed. "Hmm, now I recall that's what I

did with it. We got rid of a lot of stuff when we moved to the penthouse."

Braham smiled kindly. "Seems there are some things you just can't get rid of, however hard you try."

Diego glanced at his guitar. "Guess so!" He placed it beside his pack and said, "I'm resuming my Camino. Seems all I need now is a guitar case." Then he stepped over to Brahim and hugged him. It was a brief embrace, but it was long enough for Diego to sense Brahim's vigour and lust for life.

They stepped back from each other and with a glint in his eye, Brahim said, "It came in one I'm sure, I'll look in the basement, and see if I can find it. Then I'll prepare some breakfast."

"Too much!" Diego grinned. "But I won't say no."

"And let me help you with your gear."

Diego opened out his arms and pleaded, "Come on, I can manage it." But already Brahim had looped a strap of Diego's backpack over his shoulder and was heading out the door with it. Left there, Diego stepped over to the table and reached for his Stetson and placed it on his head. Then he removed his wedding ring from his finger and wrapped it in a handkerchief, which he stuffed into a pocket of his jeans.

He closed the balcony door and giving the river a cursory glance, noticed workmen had arrived at the bridge and were removing the scaffolding. Diego had arranged to meet Wilfred at the quay, but first, he'd join Brahim for that final breakfast. He collected his guitar and left the room.

Diego had barely exchanged more than a few words with Wilfred about his changing fortunes when two pilgrims joined them at the quay. One of them was a burly American with a patchy, sandy beard, whom Diego figured was in his mid-twenties, and the other pilgrim was a middle-aged Irish-man. Both were eager to cross the river.

Wilfred shrugged upon noticing Diego's raised eyebrows. "Well, it's a fine day for walking," said Diego. "Best I get on too."

They all boarded the little ferry. Wilfred nodded at Diego as he passed him the guitar case. His father's old case was scuffed and looked old. However, its brass latches were firm, and its crimson fabric remained intact. Diego's guitar was satisfactorily protected for the journey ahead.

Wilfred steered the boat in the diagonal upstream direc-tion, viewing the bend in the river and thinking about how his ferry business was about to change. Though it was no more than a casual thought, as he knew not to give too much grandeur to business plans, aware that all businesses were subject to the cyclical laws of the universe. He smiled serenely and continued rowing with steady hands.

When the ferry turned in the middle of the river, Diego felt the upwind breeze across his face and he had an urge to open his guitar case. Casually, he plucked a high note on the guitar, and a ripple spread across the river's surface as if the vibrating string was whispering to the water. A cormorant popped up from under the water, breaking the surface, and Diego shut the case and glanced across at the other pilgrims in the boat. They too were observing the river and the bird. Seeing their faces, Diego thought of all the pilgrims he'd rowed across the river and all the others he'd met along the Camino path.

The restaurateurs, hoteliers, fishermen, monks, prostitutes, artists, merchants, students, girlfriends, husbands and wives. Everyone was seeking something and looking for the anchor of others to give them a home and a sense of belonging. In that moment of reflection Diego grasped that was what Mari had been for him – his emotional crutch. The woman who had most reminded him of his deceased mother. As Diego crossed the Miño, he realised all his life he had been drowning in fear. Life's river for so many people was a current of fear. Though there were some among us who could reflect all such inner fears – embracing the darkest, but also the brightest places too.

Certainly, Paco, Camarón and the best *flamencos* had that gift. Although Diego recognised that even if he might have touched that source too, it had never been more than just a fleeting gesture. He knew it for sure because as he peered down into the river attempting to see into its depths, it remained a dark green, uncharted mass. But the river was also a place where the past could be forgotten. Diego placed a hand in his pocket and pulled out the handkerchief with his wedding ring wrapped inside it. Its white gold was untarnished and he gave it a last look before dropping it into the water and turning his attention to the approaching riverbank ahead.

They reached the other side and as soon as Diego stepped out of the ferry, everything felt different. He sensed an immediate kinship with his fellow passengers. They assisted each other in collecting their packs from the ferry, and then the Irishman politely bid everyone a *"Buen camino,"* before marching off towards a path and the continuing trail, whereas the young American waited further up the bank for Diego as he was saying his farewells to Wilfred. Diego and Wilfred hesitated as they stood before each other. Both men felt their time together had been too short. Yet they both understood the road they shared had come to a fork and they had to go their separate ways.

Wilfred broke the silence with a hearty laugh as he looked down at Diego's feet and his former walking shoes. "So, you're going to put my shoes to the test this time?"

Diego grinned. "Well. I'm hoping you didn't con me, 'cause they're the only shoes I own now. And what about you? Not once have I seen you wearing my old boots."

"Well sir," Wilfred replied as he bent his knees, put a foot out and switched his view to his tatty Nikes. "I'll be ditching these at the Rotary Club's annual dance. They've just invited me."

Diego winked. "When you're with a pretty *señora*, just remember whose shoes you'll be dancing in."

"Your shoes, my friend, but always my moves," replied Wilfred laughing again.

"Absolutely," said Diego holding out his hand to say goodbye.

However, Wilfred reacted by pulling Diego towards him and into a bear hug. As they embraced Diego was reminded of the farmer in Wilfred. He was a strong man who abided by the signs of nature. Afterwards, Wilfred went back to the boat and from under a seat pulled out his waterproof poncho, which he'd wrapped into a ball, and passed it over to Diego.

"What about you, brother?" asked Diego gratefully receiving his gift.

Wilfred smiled. "I plan to get a boat with roof. Remember what I said about the rain here."

"And what's this you've wrapped in it?" asked Diego feeling some metal object at the centre of the balled-up poncho. Wilfred grinned, and Diego unwrapped the poncho to reveal the coffee pot, camping stove and a cup.

"I know how you like your coffee in the morning," said Wilfred, his smile widening into a large grin.

Diego shook his head and smiling said, "*Gracias.*" Then he placed the poncho and the coffee equipment inside his pack and turned towards the American. He called up at him, "Do you think the Camino passes through the town?" He confirmed it did with a nod, and Diego continued, "Fancy a coffee, then?" The man smiled and nodded again. With that, Diego shouldered his backpack, grabbed his guitar case and headed towards the American. However, just before reaching him, Diego paused and looked over his shoulder to take a final look at his friend. Wilfred was stretching out an oar and pushing the boat away from the quay. Diego smiled and waved, but Wilfred didn't see him – his attention had already shifted to rowing the boat back to Valença.

Diego turned and continued up the riverbank. Arriving beside the American he stretched out his hand and asked, "What's your name, *amigo*?"

"Chris," replied the man shaking Diego's hand.

"*Mucho gusto*, I'm Diego. So you're American?"

"Yep. From California."

"Man, you're a long way from home."

"Not really. Not when God is all around us."

They continued up the path leading to the town, talking on the way, Diego learning that the Camino was taking Chris to a seminary in Santiago. Ordinarily, Diego shied away from religious conversation, but Chris didn't fit his image of most aspiring priests. He was wearing a Pink Floyd T-shirt, and with his wild beard, he looked more like a biker who'd just got off his Harley Davidson motorbike. There was something mischievous about Chris, and Diego was glad he had asked him to join him for coffee.

23

GALICIA

There were several cafés and *tabernas* in Tui's main plaza, and Diego and Chris had chosen one offering them a good view of the Sunday morning activity. They were smoking at their table and relaxing into the morning, Diego observing the clouds gathering in the west behind the bell tower of the church. More rain was on the way at some point. Children were running wildly around the plaza and family and friends were gathering together. Firm handshakes and polite greetings were a part of their ritual, although their voices soon became louder as coffee made way for a beer, or something stronger. Then a couple, ambling arm in arm, caught Diego's attention. He sat up straight in his chair to take a better look at them. The man was short and stocky and wearing a crisp short-sleeved shirt. The woman was petite, wearing a bright floral dress, and Diego figured she was in her early to mid-thirties.

The lovers passed close to where they were sitting and they reminded Diego of his mamá and papá, strolling along the plaza of his old village on a Sunday morning. *Could it be them?* he wondered. *The Camino is very mysterious and provides many messages.* Sensing the attention Diego was giving them, the woman glanced around, smiled and said politely, *"Buenos días"*, and the elderly man turned his head and nodded. It wasn't them, and Diego responded with a tip of his hat. The woman wore her hair longer and was taller than his deceased mother, and although the man looked older than his partner, there was not the same age gap as he recalled there had been between his parents.

Their waiter came over, and after setting down their coffees and hearing Chris' American accent, he asked him where he was from. Distracted, Diego took his eye off the passing couple and when he looked back around, he saw they were now in a far corner of the plaza, beside a children's playground. He took a breath and said inwardly, *Let it go, man.* Then he lost sight of them as the sun blurred his vision and the couple were lost amongst the parents and children. The waiter was still chatting with Chris, and when he asked them if they wanted anything else, Chris ordered a *cerveza*. When the waiter left them, Diego raised an eyebrow and said, "Chris, they let you drink as well as smoke?"

Chris leaned back in his chair and his beard ruffled across his round cheeks as he grinned. "You mean the seminary?" Diego nodded slightly while grinning and Chris replied, "They seem more concerned about us smoking than drinking."

"Hmm, I'm not sure I quite get that."

"It's God's blood!" Chris looked doubtfully at his beer. "Well, it's shaping up to be a hot day." Diego laughed and Chris added, "Got to grab your moments to relax when you can. Training to be a priest is stressful."

"Especially as you have to forfeit so much, such as sex and marriage, no?"

Chris briefly pondered the question as he took a drag on his cigarette. "God's love is enough for me."

Diego scratched his chin. "Hmm, but why the Church, why not Buddhism, for example?"

"Buddy… All religions are about faith in one's fellow brother. It's just that Christianity is the one I know the most about."

Diego still didn't quite know what to make of Chris and his thinking. Unlike some of the young Americans he'd met on the music scene, he wasn't cocky. On the contrary, he was easy-going; yet there was that rebel lurking inside him. Still, his faith seemed sincere. Diego decided to ponder on Chris' words before he delved deeper. He stubbed out his cigarette into the ashtray and finished his coffee. Chris drank the remains of his beer and was ready to walk too.

The Camino trail took them out of the plaza, down a steep hill and along a single-lane street lined by stone houses. In the driveway of one house, a stout elderly *señora* wearing a vintage apron over a blue dress was cooking pork and chicken on a barrel barbeque. She returned Diego and Chris' smiles with a tight-lipped smile, as she kept one eye on the meat. At the side of the house was a little vegetable plot, which her old husband was attending to whilst he waited for lunch. The front door to their house was ajar and a breeze wafted the lace door curtain, revealing a front room of knick-knacks and family photos.

Before long, the Camino edged alongside a bridge spanning a main road. The day was heating up, and Diego paused to undo a couple of shirt buttons and roll up his sleeves; thereafter the path veered right and into dense woodland, and they trampled over moist acorns and pinecones. Raised slatted walkways led them across marshland and streams, and as they approached a clearing beside another footbridge, the woeful sound of Galician bagpipes nearby filled the moist air. The source of the music was a lone piper, and along with some other pilgrims, they stopped walking beside a stone cross to listen to him. The man was tall and youthful. Yet his Celtic folk music was old in origin and when he completed a song, everyone placed some coins in a basket at his feet.

This prompted Chris to gesture at Diego's guitar case. "Why don't you accompany him?" Diego looked hesitant. "Come on," urged Chris. "It'd be great to hear you play."

"No, this is his patch," replied Diego as he stooped and threw some coins into the basket.

As they left, and from over his shoulder, they heard the piper shouting after them, "Diego el Relámpago. *¡Gracias!*"

Diego jerked his head around in surprise and yelled back. "It's just Diego... now." The piper acknowledged him with a nod of his head and a tilt of his bagpipe. Diego followed Chris across the bridge and they walked in silence for a little while, before Chris said, "Was that a stage name the piper was referring to?"

"Kind of. More of a nickname, Spaniards love nicknames."

"So you're famous?"

"Some people thought I was. And I could have ended up living in that world for the rest of my days. But with that life, I'd always be hiding away in bars and loathing myself."

"Hmm, like running away from God."

"So do you want to know some more flamenco nicknames? Some are ridiculous..."

Chis smiled. "For sure."

As they continued through the woodland Diego shared some of the more colourful nicknames he could think of. Camarón de la Isla – shrimp from the island; Tomatito – little tomato; el Torta – pancake; El Mojama – salt-cured tuna; el Borrico (donkey) de Jerez, and El Perro (dog) de Paterna.

Chris laughed. "That's a lot of food and animals in those names!"

"Well, we Spanish love food and animals!"

Their walk continued in good humour and the morning passed quickly. They stopped for lunch and ate a generous salad grown from the café's vegetable garden. During the afternoon they walked along country lanes lined by stone walls, behind which were small plots of recently picked grapevines, tall corn storks and pumpkins the size of beach balls. Springing from around the stones were hydrangeas, bougainvillaea and lilies, damp and vibrant.

As the afternoon leaned into the evening, Diego turned to Chris and said, "Man, only love could have created this land; call that God or otherwise. I just wish more people would experience it."

"Yep, it's breathtaking," acknowledged Chris, as he glanced across at the valley.

Diego continued talking, "I can see how the Church might help people to realign themselves with this beautiful creation. But religion has suffered from scandals and doesn't have the best reputation with certain people. And for some, teenagers especially, Instagram and Tiktok seem to be a new religion. So how do you keep the faith?"

They rounded a bend in the hill and arrived into the hamlet of Veigadaña, rich with the sweet smell of burning firewood spiralling upwards from the chimneys of several cottages. Chris didn't immediately answer the question, he was eyeing a modern *albergue* further up the road. They reached the hostel, and paused outside, contemplating whether to call it quits for the day. The garden was lively with pilgrims and workers from local timber yards, eating and drinking. Diego was about to make the case for staying the night there, when the sounds of heaving panting and slow plodding footsteps from behind distracted them.

They wheeled around to see a man dragging a foot and struggling with a large red roller suitcase, which was pulling to one side. With shoulders arched, and head bent, he concentrated on moving forward with each step. He stopped and looked up at them from under his crumpled baseball cap as he wiped his sweating brow with a handkerchief. The man was short and thin but for a potbelly pushing against his tight-fitting pullover. Grey flecks peppered his dark, unshaven chin. He looked to be in his fifties, although his exhaustion made him appear older.

"Hey, where you heading, *señor*?" asked Chris.

Pausing, the man shook his head and said in Portuguese, "I don't speak English."

Diego interjected and repeated Chris' question in Portuguese.

"Santiago," mumbled the man.

Diego and Chris glanced at each other and their looks suggested they were equally as surprised at the man's response.

"Where did you start your pilgrimage?" asked Diego.

"In Lisbon."

"He's made it all the way from Lisbon," Diego explained to Chris.

"Unbelievable," said Chris. "He's already walked over five hundred kilometres!"

Diego nodded. "But he looks done."

"Ask him if he intends to stay here for the night," urged Chris. Diego turned to the man and asked him the question.

"No *senhor*, Santiago is very far and I must keep walking while I can," he said, looking ahead at the road, which continued uphill. The man pulled his suitcase towards him, and departed, saying, "*Boa noite.*"

"*Buenas noches*," said Diego politely, not knowing how else to react.

However, Chris had interpreted the situation and said plainly, "We must help him." He walked over to the limping man, gestured up the hill and took hold of the handle of his weighty suitcase.

Diego glanced back at the *albergue* but strode forward to catch up with Chris and the limping man. Chris introduced himself, as did Diego, but the man didn't respond as he was focusing on making his way up the hill; filling the silence Chris remarked, "It's a steep climb ahead."

"It is?" responded Diego.

"Yep, according to the app," he replied, tapping his smartwatch with a finger.

"Okay," sighed Diego as he tightened his grip around the handle of his guitar case.

"So do you know how far is it to Santiago from here?"

"Funny you should say that; I know exactly."

"And how far?"

"101.14 kilometres."

"That's very precise!"

Chris grinned and nodded back at a stone Camino marker on the roadside they'd just passed. Below the yellow arrow on a brass plating was printed: 'Km 101.140.' "Always good to look down, as well as up."

Diego half-smiled. "Well, let me know when you get too tired, and we'll swap loads."

"Buddy, that might be sooner than you think. It's hard work. I think one of the wheels isn't turning?"

"Let's take a look at it."

They stopped and Diego turned the suitcase on its side and found the damaged wheel. He tried to spin it but it would only rotate halfway around.

Diego looked up at Chris. "Do you have one of those fancy penknives with a screwdriver?"

"I do."

"Thought you might."

"How did you know?" said Chris retrieving his penknife from his pack and handing it to Diego.

Diego winked. "You're American."

Then he went about removing the plastic wheel. He unscrewed the rivet and found the washer was cracked and catching on the wheel. He discarded the washer and thought for a moment, then found his arnica gel and proceeded to rub the gel onto the rivet, before replacing the wheel.

"Was that some kind of anti-inflammatory medicine?"

asked Chris curiously as Diego dropped the arnica back in his pack.

"Yep, it's miraculous for healing," replied Diego as he spun the wheel. Grinning he added, "A good lubricant too, it seems."

Seeing the wheel turning freely the limping man said, "*Obrigada!*" Thank you. Then he resumed walking.

After a while climbing the steep hill and noticing the limping man was dropping further behind them, Diego and Chris stopped to catch their breaths. When the man caught them up, he cleared his throat and said in Portuguese, "My name is Guilherme and as a child I had polio. That's why I have a bad leg." Diego smiled sympathetically. Then he translated his words into English so Chris could understand.

Chris was silent for a moment as he gathered his thoughts, and then he said, "Some are destined to be always swimming hard against the most treacherous of currents, such is life. But a few keep going, regardless, however tough the struggle, believing there is something better for them waiting on the other side. Reaching that side must be wonderful for them. Arriving in that unexplored place that most of us will never experience. It's extraordinary optimism." He turned his gaze towards Guilherme. "Buddy, I think those people must be God's chosen ones."

Diego nodded seriously at Chris before he translated his words into Portuguese. Hearing Chris' impromptu sermon seemed to lift Guilherme, as he stood a little straighter. Guilherme then said, "For ten years I had been caring for my sick mother who had Alzheimer's. But last month she died and I am now taking her ashes along the Camino to Santiago. She had once made the pilgrimage, and it was the one thing she could still remember in her last years. The Camino and Galicia's autumn leaves continued to remain vivid in her memory. You see she was originally from Galicia, and it was her final wish that I scatter her ashes into the autumn winds outside

Santiago's cathedral. Walking the Camino has always seemed a fantasy for me, but my mother's faith in the pilgrimage is what's been keeping me going."

Diego glanced to his left, noticing some of the leaves on the trees were turning russet, in contrast to the evergreen pines. He also realised they were almost at the top of the hill as he observed the treeline ahead. He pondered some on Guilherme's story. It was sad, yet he didn't feel sorry for him. Guilherme was his equal; no, he was more than his equal, as his struggle was inspiring him to keep walking and lift himself higher. Diego turned back to face his companions and said, "How you doing? It won't be that long before it's dark."

Guilherme coughed. "Actually, I'm not feeling so good. I feel a little hot and my leg is aching. I think I'm done."

Chris looked at Diego. "Is he okay?"

"I'm not sure," replied Diego, before he turned his attention to Guilherme. "No further today?"

"No, no further at all. I don't think I can reach Santiago. My leg has never felt this bad before!"

Diego looked back up the path and towards the brow of the hill and then said to Chris. "It looks like there's a clearing at the top. Maybe we'll find somewhere to stay, perhaps there's a shelter or something?" Diego explained to Guilherme what he'd just said in English, and then added, "Do you think you can make it just a little bit further? We're nearly at the top."

Guilherme removed his cap and ran a hand through his thinning strands of hair. He felt a little cooler and said, "I can try."

They continued climbing the hill, Diego taking Guilherme's arm as he leaned into him, and within a couple of minutes, they reached the top. A van was parked beside the track, and there was a picnic table in the clearing among the trees, sitting at which was a familiar figure. Chris and Diego recognised the man immediately because resting on the table beside his camping stove were the man's bagpipes. Guilherme recognised him too, having also passed by him later in the day, and, as they approached him, the piper looked up from his bowl of pasta.

"*Buenas noches*, pilgrims. Are you hungry?"

"We are," said Diego. "And we need to rest."

The piper smiled. "I might be able to help you with that too. Please join me." They joined the piper around the picnic table and nodding at his van he said, "My name is Mateo and this is my home for the moment." Mateo explained he was spending his time driving between the different Camino paths in Galicia, busking and helping the pilgrims in any way he could. Last year he too had walked the Camino and this was his way of giving something back and earning a little money. And as soon as he learned Guilherme was struggling, he immediately offered him his bed in the van and stated he also had a tent where there would be enough space for Diego, Chris and himself to sleep. He also mentioned that in the morning he could drive Guilherme to Santiago if he wished.

Mateo fetched some more food from his van and soon everyone was enjoying his recipe of Ibérico ham and pasta. Afterwards, Diego put his coffeepot on the stove and cupping mugs of steaming coffee they talked some more. From where they were sitting on the hill, they could see the sunset, a fiery blaze above the ocean, bleaching the cloud base saffron. Mateo pointed to the northwest. "Over there is Finisterre, where you get the best sunsets in Spain."

Mateo mentioned Finisterre had once been considered the end of the world, and thus the tradition these days was for some pilgrims to continue their pilgrimage along the Camino Finisterre, after reaching Santiago. Pagans believed the sun died there, and it was a place where the dead and living became closer, and prayers and offerings would be made to please the gods. Nowadays pilgrims performed their own ceremonies once reaching there, such as burning their boots or swimming in the ocean. After hearing about such rituals Guilherme took a sip of his coffee, looked up at the final wisps of saffron cloud and said, "My mother's funeral was very small." He glanced at Diego's guitar case resting against the table and at the bagpipe, and then he looked over at Diego and Mateo. "Perhaps you could both play something to suit the mood so I could spread my mother's ashes here, among the trees?"

"You'll make it to Santiago," responded Diego, slightly surprised. "Come on, you've made it this far."

"Exactly, I have made it this far into Galicia, this is the place she most loved, especially along the Camino. Now the moment feels right. I think she made the request as an incentive to make me walk the Camino." Guilherme raised his arms out wide. "And look where I am, how far I have already walked." He looked at Mateo again. "Tomorrow you can drive me to Santiago, that is okay?"

Mateo nodded. "Yes of course. In Santiago, I can busk for a few days."

"In that case, I will save some ashes for Santiago." Guilherme returned his gaze to Diego. "You will accompany Mateo?"

Diego glanced at his guitar case and then at the bagpipes. He looked at Mateo and said, "It's okay if I join you in a song?"

"It would be an honour," replied the young man.

Diego didn't delay in retrieving the guitar from his case and tuning it, though, again, it only required minimum attention. Guilherme got up from the table and searched inside his suitcase for the urn containing his mother's ashes. With it in hand, he hobbled away from the table to take in the vista. Mateo retrieved his bagpipes and gestured to Diego to play.

Diego held the guitar tight against his chest and said to the piper, "No, you lead, Mateo. Play whatever suits you, and I'll do my best to follow."

Mateo tilted his head towards the mouthpiece of his bagpipe and what came from his instrument was the mournful echoes of the fateful fighting for their Galician homelands; of the widowed wives of fishermen calling out for their men and sons to return home from the unforgiving sea. It was a mantra filled with loss, of grief, and loneliness. Diego weaved in a gypsy melody just as ancient and haunting. His guitar wailed as he slapped the soundboard, and as he picked and strummed its strings, it cried and screeched with the despair of the Moors and the grief of a lover waiting for the eternal traveller.

As he listened, mesmerised by the music, Chris sensed the leaves of the trees curling and noticed a mist wafting into the valley below. He also saw near the Camino path the glint of Guilherme's urn, gilded by the final traces of the sun's rays. A spontaneous yet brief rain shower sounded like faint drumbeats as it fell onto the trees and fallen leaves, and the Celt and gypsy song cut through each other like the stormy winds off the Atlantic, and the *levanter* blowing in the Mediterranean Sea. Their music spiralled and circled to a raging crescendo, then calmed like the wind that ripples across grain fields.

Guilherme returned from the shadows and cupped his hands together, directing his attention to the two musicians. He wiped back a tear and said, *"Obrigada senhors.* Celtic kings wouldn't have had a better send-off than that."

NOT LONG AFTER, they erected Mateo's tent and everyone turned in for the night. As they slept, the murmurs on the coastline spoke to them and the bending treetops hummed in their dreams. They said to them: Strong travellers, you are as worthy as the stars and the moon. When your wanderings cease, be ready for great deeds.

The next morning after Diego and Chris had just said their

goodbyes to Guilherme and Mateo, Chris said to Diego, "You're not tempted to join them and arrive in Santiago today?"

Diego glanced up at some grey clouds and replied, "Man, it's tempting, but I want to keep walking."

Chris grinned. "Are you sure you're not religious?" He looked around Diego and up at the clouds and the coastline. "In the seminary I learn about God, but that's not where I see him."

Diego patted Chris on his shoulder. "Very profound, *amigo*. I'd keep a journal and save all those wise words for your future sermons."

Mateo turned on the engine of his van and Diego and Chris waved him and Guilherme off, yelling after them in unison, "*¡Buen camino!*"

Diego and Chris continued along the track and as the sun rose over the treetops Chris said, "Now that's faith for you!"

"It's like Guilherme always knew he'd make it to Santiago, one way or another."

"Yep," said Chris.

There was no need for Diego to press Chris anymore about his loyalty to the Church, appreciating that faith in its purest form was about finding the positives in life.

24

THE CAMINO OF LIFE

Their walk took them towards the coast and a misty rain fell on them for most of the day. However, the walking was good. Bridges took them across coastal inlets and the rivers were flush with migratory sea trout. They stopped several times to brush off the rain and fuel up on meaty *bocadillo* baguettes, coffee and cigarettes.

At one bar they retreated inside to dry off and drink another coffee. Their view from the window was of a multi-arched medieval stone bridge and for some time they observed the various pilgrims in their waterproofs striding across it. After a while, Chris asked, "So why are you walking the Camino, Diego?"

"Because I couldn't find any reason not to."

Chris smiled. "Resistance is futile."

Diego laughed. "That sounds like a line out of *The Terminator*. But yes, that about sums it up. I have a calling to return to Santiago."

"Well, buddy, each step is taking you closer." Chris didn't enquire anymore about Diego's reasons or past life. He had already felt Diego's determination to reach Santiago and had sensed he was still figuring out a few things in his mind.

"But what about you, Chris? I know this is kind of a religious pilgrimage for you. But why Spain and the Camino in particular?"

Chris set his cup down. "I thought you'd never ask."

"I can feel a sermon coming on!"

"Don't worry, mine is a simple story... I was a football player who crashed and burned. Not a soccer player, but an American football player."

"I understand," answered Diego.

"I was about to turn pro, but in a college game I suffered a life-threatening back injury that ended the dream."

"That's tough, man. It must have been really bad?"

"Yep, it hurt. I was tackled hard in a game and, to cut a long story short, I was flipped backwards and my spine was almost bent in half. The next two years of my life were spent going in and out of surgery and physio. It's a miracle I'm walking, frankly. The only thing that kept me going was my faith. Though I admit, for about a year after the injury had healed, I didn't leave my parents' house, not wanting to do anything or see anyone. My parents are religious and they keep a Bible in every room. For that year I found myself reading through it several times from their lounge sofa. It was much better than TV. And you know what I discovered?"

"Go on," said Diego.

"The teachings of God are easily misrepresented because they were written in a time that no longer exists today. So people are very confused by them. I realised the way to make it relatable was to know today's people. That's when I decided it was time to get off the couch and know the world. I figured one way to do that was to walk through some foreign lands and towns. So here I am in my second year of seminary training in Santiago and walking the Camino during the autumn break."

"Wow! It might have been easier to become an accountant or lawyer, as you have a college education, no?"

"If I'd stayed on the couch any longer that's probably what would have happened. As time went by, I would have forgotten about my miracle and my second chance at walking. The more we ponder on our dreams and destinies, the less likely we are to fulfil them, I think."

Diego glanced out of the window, seeing that the pilgrims now crossing the bridge weren't wearing waterproofs. "Well, we better keep walking in that case; I've had my fill of lawyers lately."

Chris looked at Diego curiously, though remained silent as they paid for their coffees and collected their packs.

Making good time they later arrived in the small city of Pontevedra. At its heart was a medieval centre of plazas and pedestrianised avenues, alive with evening crowds. The place reminded Diego of León, where he'd first had the courage to busk in a public square along the Camino, all those years ago. It felt tempting to try again. However, Chris was keen to get to the hotel he'd booked in advance, hoping he'd be able to switch to a room with twin beds. They were in luck. The shower steamed in the ensuite and although their room was above a compact plaza, tightly packed with vibrant restaurants and bars, both pilgrims knew that sleeping would come easily that night.

Refreshed and in dry clothes, Chris persuaded Diego to come with him to the pilgrim's mass, and although Diego felt the urge to stop off at one of the pavement cafés, he continued to stride alongside Chris, who didn't want to miss the start of the service. Mass was being held in a Baroque chapel, and before entering it, Diego felt compelled to walk around the building. Circumnavigating it, he realised its foundations were shaped like a scallop shell. Outside the main doorway, he took several steps back to fully take in the full majesty of the building, the yellowing stonework creating a striking effect against the grey evening sky. It was time to go inside;

he followed Chris up the steps and they sat on a pew at the back.

Diego's eyes darted around the space as he observed the intricate details offered in dedication to the Camino, from the various scallop shell carvings to St. James above the altar, but he was aware of the pilgrims too. Some looked in worse shape than others; noticing it through their worn shoes, tears or weather-beaten faces, yet in that moment of the mass, all were being nourished by the same invisible energy. And that's when he acknowledged what the church had to offer, with its ability to heal, and he finally gave it a break. Of course, Diego recognised it wasn't perfect, because like most institutions it is organised by man. But he now saw that mankind was striving to improve, and the only way to go forward was to keep the faith and keep walking.

When the mass had finished and they were descending the steps of the chapel, Diego turned to Chris and said, "*Gracias.* I think I can be alone now."

"You want to walk on your own?"

"Maybe, but that's not what I meant," replied Diego, nodding over his shoulder. "In there, at the mass, it confirmed that I've never been able to face being alone, even before meeting my wife, Mari. And because of that, I've always sought the approval of others. Fame was perhaps the epitome of that, but I've been fooling myself. I can be alone. Everything is one. For example, the Church is the Camino. As are the trees, birds, fish, ants, sun, wind, bars, *albergues*, the people who live along its paths, and the pilgrims, all are a part of it. We are never really alone! I believe my music has been trying to tell me that too." Diego looked Chris directly in the eyes, and said, "Does that make much sense?"

Chris scratched his beard thinking and then smiled. "That pretty much cuts to the chase, Diego. I must remember those words for a future sermon, too. If you don't mind me using them?"

"Of course not." Diego found himself stepping back up a couple of the church steps and taking in the view of the plaza ahead. The grey stone, the movement of people, the chatter around the cafés, pigeons, a curious cat. It was a moment in time, a moment in history, and his senses were alert to it all.

RAIN AND BROOMSTICKS

Market stalls were opening in the plaza, people were off to work, walking their dogs, sweeping their door-ways. From their breakfast table and through the window of the hotel Diego and Chris watched them go about the routines of life with curious fascination. They noticed the early pilgrims filing past them, too, flags on their packs, walking sticks tapping off the steps of their day's journey. Eager to get going too, Diego and Chris paid their bill and got back on the road.

They walked under a low, grey sky, through the old town and over a wide pedestrian bridge. By the time they'd reached the city suburbs, intermittent drops of rain had begun to fall on them.

"Looks like it's going to pour down," said Chris retrieving his rain jacket from his pack.

"*Sí*, looks like it's finally coming."

Diego pulled out his poncho, put his hat into his pack and pulled the cape over himself and his guitar. They resumed walking, but within a couple of hundred metres, the sun broke through the clouds, and no more rain fell.

"Reckon your *Señor* up there is playing games with us?" said Diego, pulling off his poncho.

"Possibly, but look at that!" replied Chris pointing above a railway bridge towards a double rainbow.

"Whoa, wow! I have never seen anything like that before," Diego exclaimed, observing the bright arches against the patchy sky.

"In the Bible, they say double rainbows are messages from God," noted Chris.

"Really? What kind of messages?"

"New beginnings, peace and redemption. Those kinds of messages." Chris studied the rainbow some more. "Or perhaps it means that you should follow the road you've chosen."

Diego smiled serenely. "Not sure I'll ever be a regular in church, but I'd drop in for one of your sermons."

"Well, you'll have to wait a few years yet, buddy. But I'll keep a seat for you."

They continued towards the bridge and just before it crossed over their path, the road forked. On the roadside was a stump with a Camino arrow pointing in the direction of the left fork, and next to it was a large signboard with a map. It displayed information about an alternative route to Santiago, via: Variante Espiritual, a route of three stages, before it rejoined the final stage of the Camino Portugués.

"Looks interesting?" remarked Diego, his eyes widening. "And its final section is via a ferry."

"It does, but it would add an extra day."

"In a rush?" said Diego.

"I have an important appointment with God in Santiago. But if you fancy taking that route, don't let me hold you back."

"*Bien*, arriving by boat doesn't sound bad, especially now that you've got me thinking about rainbows."

"Take the rainbow path then and we'll catch up in Santiago."

Diego nodded. "Okay, sounds like a plan – where will I find you?"

"The seminary is housed in the monastery of San Martiño Pinario – you won't miss it; it's huge and is in the centre of the city."

They departed with a firm handshake, Diego taking the left road and Chris continuing right and passing under the bridge. Diego's road headed northwest towards the coast and within a couple of hours, he was walking along a path hugging an estuary and heading towards the village of Combarro nestling above the water's edge.

He found himself going around in circles as Combarro's lanes meandered like a maze past old stone-terraced fisherman's cottages. However, when he paused beside a stone cross with an altar table, at a junction of sorts, he smelled fish grilling in the salty air. The aroma led him down a narrow lane to rows of fish restaurants above the harbour and past artisan shops selling various trinkets. Hanging in the doorways of the shops were witch dolls riding broomsticks. In front of the restaurants were wood-fired barbecues grilling rows of fresh fish. Diego sat at a table beside the barbeques and was soon lunching on mackerel and *padrón* peppers.

Halfway through eating, the rain came. Light at first, splashing delicately onto the parasols, then quicker and persistent. Water streamed across the paving stones, around the table legs, gushing like waterfalls over the sea wall. Diego pulled his chair further into the table and under the parasol. Staring across the dark bay he surveyed the steep hills he would next need to climb, disappearing behind the swathes of rain. The idea of drinking again and for the rest of the afternoon suddenly appealed. However, he fought the temptation to do so. Particularly now that he was on a budget. If he was lucky, after paying for lunch, he might have enough money left over to cover a night or two in an *albergue* or hostel. His only option was to carry on and stop at the next pilgrim lodgings along his path.

After lunch, Diego pulled on his cape and shivered as the cold autumn rain splashed onto him. Leaving the alleyways, he edged along a main highway looking for a sign to reunite him with the Camino. But in the gloom and with his head bent against the rain it was hard to find one. Passing a modern hotel, he came across a rain-soaked man with a backpack about to enter the hotel. They spoke briefly, the man advising that further along, Diego would find the Camino climbing into the hills. The man had decided to stay for the night and resume his walk when the rain had passed.

Diego found a yellow arrow Camino marker just a couple of hundred meters ahead, pointing in the direction of a tarmac track, rising steeply away from the main road and cutting through tall hardwood trees growing into the mountain ridges. It was an arduous climb and at every bend, Diego thought he was seeing the treeline and the top. However, the crest of the ridge remained elusive and he continued walking, occasionally ducking under the trees to shelter or drink some water. Within a couple of hours, he finally reached the top. Diego's timing was good too – the rain had eased into a drizzle and there was a lookout that provided a misty view of the estuary and village below. The world looked tiny, almost insignificant, and Diego realised he'd made good progress.

He shook the rain off and after removing his cape, inspected his guitar inside the case. It remained dry and with a half-smile Diego rapped his knuckles against its spruce body and quipped, "*Amigo*, we've made it to higher ground."

The road levelled out into a chalky track cutting through gorse, which was dotted with sporadic yellow flowers. Late afternoon the rain came hard again. Diego looked with disdain at the grey clouds from under the brim of his hat and retrieved his cape. Eventually, the path turned downhill and Diego had the sense that it wouldn't be too long before a village would greet him on the other side of the woods. He followed a brook flowing fast with rainwater and trudged on, knowing there was nothing else to do but continue walking. After a while, he left the woods, and his path hit a country road.

He passed a couple of large houses and further along the road was an old monastery beside a restaurant. Diego entered its cloister through an open archway and approached the main entrance. He found the door locked. He put his ear to the wood but heard only silence. Asking about accommodation at the restaurant was his next option and stepping inside, he found it lively with pilgrims and friendly staff. A lanky Polish man with his sociable daughter, equally tall, who spoke English, sent him in the direction of the local *albergue*. It was to be found just a kilometre or so out of the village and off the main road.

Although he endured a long kilometre, the girl's directions were accurate, and he arrived feeling in good spirits. However, his heart sank when the hostel's stressed warden, a middle-aged woman with an austere face, and gripping a mop, turned Diego away, saying it was already over its capacity and she would be breaking the rules if she admitted anyone else. Paying no attention to Diego's sodden state, all she could offer were directions to a private hostel, some five kilometres further along the pilgrim path and on the other side of another woodland.

The woman didn't hear Diego's, "*Gracias*," as she'd immediately marched off with her mop in hand, her mind on some puddle. Diego tilted his Stetson against the rain, sighed and carried on down the road, his jeans as dark and heavy with rain as the sky. At a crossroads, he came to a stile marked with a pilgrim arrow that pointed towards a meadow and into a wood. He looked up through the rain at a three-quarter moon faintly visible through the low cloud. Then he climbed over the stile, crossed the rain-soaked meadow and entered the woods.

OLD AMIGOS

The Camino followed a fast-flowing stream that cut between mossy boulders. Thunder began rumbling in the distance; Diego pulled his cape closer to him, and walked tentatively along the slippery stone path. The route passed by the remains of stone watermills, and in the sudden flashes of lightning, he could see they were in different states of repair. The sky darkened further and the thunder roared above. Diego winced, sensing the storm was drawing closer. He had no desire to be among the trees or finding his way in the dark for much longer. His fingers tightened around the handle of his guitar case. He quickened his pace, and in the interludes of brightness, Diego saw wisps of smoke coming from the chimney of one of the ancient mills.

He pushed on against the roaring of the wind and the rain lashing through the trees. Suddenly there was a blaze of light in his path, immediately followed by a crashing sound, and he fell backwards. Diego's backside and pack absorbed most of the fall. Holding firmly onto his guitar case, he sat back up, smelling smouldering wood. Out of the gloom, he saw a shadowy figure ahead, rushing from the restored mill towards the broad tree that had just been split in two by the lightning bolt and right in front of Diego's path. Diego stood back up on shaky legs. Dazed but unharmed, he called out to the figure. "*Hola*, hey!"

The person glanced over their shoulder but didn't reply. Instead, the figure turned to look at the fallen tree. It had split close to its base and fallen across the stream, bridging both banks. The blurry figure leaned a broad shoulder into it and ran his hand across its bark. He appeared male and as thick as the tree trunk. *Perhaps a forest ranger*, Diego thought. The thunder began to fade, moving northwards, and Diego gathered himself together. He approached the man, took another couple of breaths, and then said, "Reckon the storm has passed."

The man paused, slowly lifted his hand from the tree and then turned around to face Diego. Though it was dark, patches of moonlight slanted through the trees, providing enough light for Diego to recognise the man standing in front of him. His greying beard shimmered silver in the pale light, and although there were more wrinkles around his eyes, they still maintained their chestnut glow. There was no doubt that he was facing Leonardo.

"Diego?" said Leonardo calmly.

Diego tipped his hat behind his head and wiped his face dry with a shirt cuff. "*Sí señor*. In the flesh."

"I believe it is you, Diego! But look at you; you're wet to the bone. Let's get you inside."

Leonardo led Diego away from the tree and towards the mill. He pulled open its wooden door and Diego felt like he was passing through the entrance of a cave, though it was reasonably bright inside. It was lit by a miner's lantern hanging on a peg in the wall. The space was compact; along one wall was a camp bed and against the adjacent wall was a camping stove and storage boxes. In a corner of the mill was a wood burner and in the centre of the room was the round grinding stone, which served as a table of sorts.

"You live here?" asked Diego.

"It's just temporary, but it could be home," answered Leonardo bending down to the wood burner and adding a couple of logs to it. The wood hissed and crackled, and the fire roared up; Leonardo went over to the camping stove, lit a ring and placed a kettle on it. "I'll make coffee." Then he grinned, "And I've got a little something I can add to keep the chill at bay."

Diego smiled. "Thought you might, but I'll just stick to the coffee." Leonardo nodded and Diego said, "That was a close shave with the tree."

"Hmm, indeed. Very strange meeting you like that!" Leonardo grinned, "Stranger still that you're passing up on some rum. But you're no crazier than before. The last time I met you in a wood, you were up a tree, looking lost, now you were almost under one! You must have some story for being back on the Camino, in this weather?"

"Guess so."

Leonardo nodded up at some pegs above the wood burner. "Hang your clothes and wet things up there, get changed and we'll catch up. How long has it been?"

"Not far off ten years, I'd say," replied Diego as he pulled off his cape, and stepped across to the wood burner with his gear.

He stood beside the fire and quickly changed into some dry clothes. After Leonardo had made the brew, he pulled the camp bed closer to the grinding stone. Diego sat on an edge of it and held out his mug as Leonardo filled it with coffee. Leonardo then sat further along the bed, poured some rum into his own coffee and they began catching up on their lives.

Leonardo spoke first, saying that after returning from Santiago it had initially been a struggle to find a job working with trees. So, when the construction trade picked up again, he felt the pressure to return to it, especially with his girl-friend and former workmates pushing him to do so. But he knew that going back to that life would end up destroying him. Soon he'd be pressured into working long hours, drinking with his colleagues, and ending up being hard on himself and everyone around him. So he left his girlfriend for good, distanced himself from his old workmates, and continued with his arboriculture studies. He paid the bills working as a delivery driver. And eventually, he got his lucky break.

It had happened when one day Leonardo was making a delivery of saplings to a vineyard, and he had met the owner, marking out a patch of land to build cabins for guests to stay overnight at the vineyard. He also wanted to plant trees to compensate for the wood used in their construction. Leonardo immediately put himself forward for the job. The vineyard owner, being a risk-taker, gave Leonardo his chance, and he oversaw the construction of the cabins as well as planting a grove of some forty trees. The proprietor was more than satisfied with Leonardo's work and subsequently introduced him to viticulture. For a couple of years, Leonardo worked at the vineyard. However, the proprietor, being well connected and aware of the shuffles of management within various agricultural departments in local government and seeing that Leonardo wanted to go further, introduced him to the right people in those departments. Those new connections gave Leonardo some forestry work, including this, his latest job.

He explained, "There are a dozen different species of trees in this woodland, and Galicia's government is now recognising the importance of protecting them. Plus, there's the stream and its habitat to maintain. Money has been granted to restore the woodlands and already we're seeing more river birds and animals returning. The watermills are the next part of the project. By restoring some of them to working order we can show the usefulness of natural waterpower. For example, we will restore this mill for cereal production."

"Noble work Leonardo, but don't you mind being out here by yourself? Look what happened with the tree, it could have landed on the mill."

"Ha, that's nature! But that only drives me on to find more ways to work with the environment and not against it."

"But you're not lonely?"

"There's no time to be lonely when you're doing what you love. Anyway, I couldn't do all this on my own. Tomorrow morning my workmates on the project will be here again. I just prefer to sleep here. I always learn something. The trees whisper ideas to me that I would never hear in the noisy towns and cities. I've come to appreciate that it's good to have a space to think clearly before people get a chance to judge your ideas, based on their own limiting beliefs." Leonardo paused and took a sip of his coffee, smiling as the rum warmed him inside. Then he glanced at the soccer shirt Diego had changed into. "Is that Sporting Lisbon?"

Diego nodded. "You know your football."

"Of course. To grow up in the Basque country is to grow up an Athletic Bilbao fan – meaning we have watched all the big clubs and best players. The great Ronaldo once wore the colours you're wearing. You hear of how he eats differently and does extra training on his own?" Diego nodded in agreement and Leonardo continued, "And although he appears to be constantly surrounded by his teammates and a media circus, he's quoted as saying he doesn't have many friends in football. I figure, unencumbered by others, he's free to pursue alternative ways to stay ahead. And look at the result – he's a goal machine!"

"*Sí*, but I'm not sure I completely follow your point?"

"Those in touch with themselves don't worry what others think and are happy in their own company. So they become relaxed in going their own way – their best way – and nothing will obstruct them. Just as water is harder than stone." Diego briefly turned his gaze toward the window as he heard the gurgle of the brook rushing over moss and stone and on its way to merge with the sea. When Diego returned his attention, Leonardo added, "Not even Ronaldo's father passing away, when he was barely more than a teenager, held him back. As it might have done for less self-aware people."

Diego felt his throat tightening and he took a sip of his coffee. Tears began to well up in his eyes as he recognized there was still an enormous obstacle in his life. Standing up, he set his mug on the grinding stone and stepped across to the wood burner. Holding his hands towards the fire he levelled up with himself. *I let go of Mari, but I still want Mamá's love.* He knew if he didn't finally come to terms with his mother's death, he would always be searching for her love, searching for it in other women, on aimless, tortuous roads, until he found nothing but his own lonely death.

Leonardo went over to the stove, aware of Diego's need for a moment to himself and said, "I'll put some stew on, that will warm you up." From one of the containers, he took out some sprigs of wild herbs and crumbled them into the pot, stirring it slowly as he added salt and pepper. When it was ready, they again took their places beside the stone table.

Leonardo handed Diego a bowl of steaming stew and receiving it, Diego sensed their friendship. In Leonardo's shelter, there was nothing to fear and he jested, "You haven't gone all vegetarian now?"

"Come on? But maybe you have with your fancy friends, in Madrid."

Diego stirred his stew with a spoon, noticing the chunks of cured ham in it "Hey, no way, Basque man. Anyway, how did you know about my life in Madrid?"

Leonardo pulled out a smartphone from under his woollen fleece. "I'm not completely Stone Age – I'm aware of YouTube."

"Well, in that case, you might have noticed I'm not so popular all of a sudden."

"I did see something…"

As they ate Diego told Leonardo about his former life and why he had returned to the Camino. They talked late into the night until the point the rain had calmed down to a gentle patter. With the fire burning low, Leonardo said, "Diego, my friend, you look tired. Go, take the bed, and get some sleep."

The only bed Diego saw in the mill was the neatly made camp bed they were sitting on. "No, no, Leonardo. You keep your bed. After walking all day and nearly being struck by lightning, the floor here will do me fine."

Leonardo glanced over at Diego's sleeping bag and clothes drying on the pegs. "Your bag is still probably damp. Either you take the bed or no one takes it."

Diego remembered the seriousness of Basque hospitality. He accepted Leonardo's offer and climbed into the camp bed. Leonardo wrapped himself in blankets, curled up on the floor and slept with his feet poking out towards the wood burner.

Diego awoke to the smell of coffee and Leonardo slicing a baguette and dropping ham into a frying pan on the stove. He jumped out of bed and went over to where his clothes were drying.

Leonardo called over his shoulder, "They're dry?"

Diego reached up to a peg for his jeans. Scrunching them, he responded cheerily, "They are!"

"Superb."

Diego pulled his jeans on and wore his shirt over the Sporting Lisbon top. Fully dressed, he went outside into the morning. He stepped through damp bracken and took a pee behind a tall tree, observing the lush flora before him and the sunlight bending through the trees. Then he noticed an otter running along the edge of the stream before it twitched its head and scurried down the bank. He went over to the stream, but the otter was gone. He washed his hands in the water, thinking: *Life is just a moment in time, but it's miraculous.*

Returning inside the hut, Leonardo handed Diego a mug

of coffee and a plate of Spanish ham and eggs. They took their breakfast outside and sat on a large rock above the stream. Words didn't seem that important, but when they did occasionally speak, it related to practicalities. Leonardo noted Diego was less than two days' walking from Santiago if he took the ferry.

"Will you stay in the mill throughout the winter?" Diego asked Leonardo.

Leonardo nodded to indicate he would, and then added, "But I will return to my village, where I still have a house, for Christmas."

"Hmm!" replied Diego in surprise.

Both friends could have sat together above the stream all morning, but Leonardo's workmates had recently arrived, and they needed help carrying materials from their van parked further along the stream at a recreational area. Diego delayed his departure to help them, but after offloading a final length of timber beam, it was time to get going and he went back to Leonardo's mill to collect his belongings.

All set, he retrieved his hat from the wall, pulled on his pack and collected his guitar case. Diego smiled at his friend. "*Amigo*, apologies, this time I forgot to play you a song. Least I should have done."

As they stepped outside, Leonardo tapped Diego softly on the shoulder and replied, "That's okay brother, we had a lot of catching up to do." Diego put his case down and hugged his friend. Their embrace was brief, but their brotherhood was everlasting.

Diego grabbed his backpack and guitar and set off again. After a couple of steps, he paused and glanced over his shoulder. Leonardo had remained in the doorway. "How can I get hold of you?" shouted Diego.

Leonardo grinned, looked up at the sky and yelled in reply, "The big man is bound to let you know!"

Diego tapped the brim of his hat with his forefinger,

nodded, and then curled the finger around a strap of his pack. Reaching the fallen tree, he raised a leg to step over it but then instead brought his foot down on top of it. The bark was rough and had dried in the early morning sun. It felt like a reliable enough bridge. He stepped onto it and crossed over to the western side of the stream.

SHADOWLESS

I t was mid-autumn now but after the rain it felt spring-like. Diego only had to make it to Vilanova de Arousa by nightfall, so he did not need to hurry. Leonardo had mentioned that the ferry would likely depart before dawn the next day to catch the high tide, as upriver the estuary was very shallow. He walked alongside several more waterways and witnessed cormorants, trout nibbling river plants, and neighbours chatting in raked fields. His ears were alert to the sounds of woodpeckers and cuckoos. The urban world remained on the periphery. The edge of a sandy beach with wind bent trees lined the pathway mid-afternoon, as he approached Vilanova de Arousa. Ahead, he saw some male pilgrims walking three abreast, their backpacks riding high on their shoulders as they crossed a footbridge over the estuary and into the harbour town. He followed after them.

Diego went to bed shortly after sundown at the town's sports centre, which doubled up as the local *albergue*. Arriving at the harbourfront before dawn, most places were still closed, apart from a bakery and Diego bought himself a couple of croissants for breakfast. Then he mounted his camping stove on the seawall and set about brewing coffee.

Drinking his coffee, he gazed across the harbour towards the early morning mist rolling in from the sea. Mentally, he traced his footsteps back to Porto and that first morning coffee with Nessie, thinking that, indeed, life was a strange miracle. Unaware at the time, that it would be his first day on the Camino Portugués. He wrapped his hands around his coffee mug as the cool sea air chilled his cheeks and wondered about Nessie. What was she doing now? Was she back with her boyfriend? He still felt ashamed about how he'd treated her. Then he found himself grinning as a cliché tickled him inside: *Wake up and smell the coffee.* He should enjoy his final day on the Camino.

Sleepy-eyed pilgrims began to gather beside the boat due to take them up river and soon its dapper skipper, Iago, arrived and ushered everyone aboard. Diego avoided the busy cabin filled with some twenty pilgrims, preferring to sit outside in the cockpit. He propped himself up against his pack and stared across the stern at the dark outlines of the town perched against crooked hills, blushed by the first hints of sunrise. The engine roared, Diego turned up his shirt collar, and Iago steered the boat out of the harbour and into the mist.

Breaks in the sea fog revealed floating platforms topped with lobster cages and fishermen with nets. Further upstream, arising out of the misty seabed were ancient stone crosses, marking bookends in the Camino story. Iago commented that the estuary had first carried St. James' boat into Galicia, and at the end of his life it also returned his martyred body from Jerusalem. Diego smiled wryly at the thought of Wilfred peddling his own version of the story.

In little over an hour, they were disembarking at a mooring near Padrón. Excitement filled the dawn air as the community of pilgrims marched through the town's medieval streets, eager to conclude their pilgrimages. Looking up from the riverbank, Diego saw some hills cutting into the skyline, and he appreciated he still had a little further to walk before he would arrive in Santiago, some twenty kilometres away.

Diego's legs remained strong and by mid-morning he was on the other side of the hills and descending through a wood of pine and eucalyptus, their shadows stretching towards Santiago. Leaving the trees behind, he viewed Santiago in the distance, and although they appeared tiny, he believed he was looking at the twin spires of the city's cathedral rising high above the rooftops into the azure sky. A pedestrian bridge over a highway led Diego into the city's suburbs, and half an hour later, he had entered the heart of Santiago's Old Town, its streets alive with pilgrims, tourists and locals going about their business. Heading for the cathedral, he noted a side street branching off his cobbled path – the one that had previously led him towards the store where he'd purchased his flamenco guitar, all that time ago, on his original Camino. "We've returned," he whispered, glancing down at the case swinging beside him.

The busy thoroughfare wound its way through the medieval town and he soon arrived at the main plaza. And there it was, the cathedral rising before him with the stone image of St. James gazing down, framed by those spires he'd viewed earlier. Diego removed his pack and sitting down to face the cathedral, craned his neck to get a better view of the building. He closed his eyes, feeling the sun warming his face. Then, the square began to echo with the chimes from the cathedral's bell tower. The tones initially brought to mind wedding bells, though the ringing was slower, deeper and more deliberate, like wide strides guiding pilgrims through the city. Then, hearing the twelfth and final chime, Diego grasped it was midday – he'd arrived just in time for the pilgrim mass.

He got up, grabbed his belongings and headed around the

side of the cathedral, remembering the mass was accessed from another entrance in a smaller plaza. Reaching the entrance, Diego saw a line of pilgrims filing through the gateway and he stepped up his pace. He hurried up the steps towards them, but at the doorway a woman stepped out of the shadows, blocking his way.

Rushing, Diego mistook her for a steward and said, "Is it my gear? Can I leave it somewhere?"

"You can leave it with me if you like?"

Immediately Diego recognised the woman's voice. He froze for a moment, before taking a step back to take a better look at her. She was hidden behind large sunglasses, but it was definitely Mari blocking his path. She removed her glasses and nervously ran a hand through her fringe. "I've been waiting for you to arrive." Underneath her cardigan, she was wearing a favourite summer dress. She went to hug Diego, but he took another step back.

"You have? But you were desperate to get divorced? I thought..."

"... Don't say anything, Diego. Please just let me explain... The owner at the pilgrim guesthouse in Valença told me you had resumed walking to Santiago." Diego's body tingled and he wanted to say something, but Mari continued talking, "When I returned to Madrid and our apartment, I didn't know what to do. It felt so empty without you. Then, when it was sold, I felt relieved and a plan came to me. I thought, no one knows you better than me; our life can go on. I now realise that all you need to do is strike out on your own, and I could be your manager. After all, I have so many contacts in Madrid and the flamenco world. What do you think?"

Diego put his case down, not quite believing what he was hearing. His eyes narrowed as he tried to read Mari's mind. She looked just as beautiful as that time they had met in El Retiro Park in Madrid, when she'd been wearing that same blue dress. It would have been so easy to try again with her and say, 'yes'. But he knew bridges had been burned and there was no going back. He took a deep breath, and said, "Are you no longer with Carlos?"

Mari bit her lower lip. "Oh, that. You knew?" Diego nodded. "It was nothing, he was there when I needed someone to talk to. It just got a bit out of hand, but only briefly. He and his friends were so old in their attitude – I could never be with someone like that. I should be thankful to him, really, as he showed me that we belong together."

"Hmm, is he seeing anyone else now?

Mari brushed her hand through her hair. "Maybe, I'm not sure? He has a tendency to be economical with the truth."

Diego knew that Carlos Pepi had a reputation as a ladies' man, as did many of the pop stars he'd met along the way. It was likely Pepi had already moved on to someone else. Mari looked lonely, but Diego knew it would be a mistake if he became her shoulder to cry on. He reached for the handle of his case and said, "I have to admit, if you'd caught me just a few weeks ago, I would have jumped at a second chance. But now I've come this far on my own, I need to keep going it alone." Diego nodded towards the doorway. "I have to go."

"You're sure?"

"I am."

Mari stepped away from the doorway. "This is it, then?"

Diego smiled fondly at Mari. "I'm truly sorry for my behaviour in the past but I feel we'll be alright." Then he walked past her towards the cathedral and he didn't look back over his shoulder. He didn't want to give her false hope, recognising it was natural to have doubt before fully committing to a new path.

As soon as he passed under its portico, an aroma, reminiscent of the fallen smouldering tree, drifted his way. Towards the transept, he witnessed the source of the smell. Swinging high above the congregation's heads and heading at considerable speed in his direction was a giant incense burner expelling billows of smoke. A pulley system and several attendants pulling hard on ropes, like church bell ringers, were operating it. They were swinging the legendary *Botafumeiro*, and Diego was reminded that he had arrived at the cathedral's mass during Holy Year when it was swung more frequently.

With everyone distracted, he edged his way towards the back and placed his pack and guitar down in a corner. He found a space on the end of a pew but remained standing. He was transfixed by the *Botafumeiro*. Its hypnotic pendulum movements, combined with the choral music echoing around the cathedral, made Diego feel a little giddy. He sat down and closed his eyes. The music and incense rolled over him and when the ritual of the Communion began, he discovered himself joining the line leading to the altar, ready to receive the bread and wine. Arriving at the front, he observed the priest dressed in a scarlet cloak embroidered with the Santiago cross and placing the bread on the tongue of the pilgrim in front. Assisting the priest with the wine was a younger man with sandy hair. He was dressed in a white robe and looked the size of a bear next to the priest.

Diego's turn came and after receiving the bread he looked up at the large man and readied himself to receive the wine. The man had a serious face and was cleanly shaven. Yet the mischievous glint in his eyes was familiar. It was Chris standing before Diego. Chris prolonged his eye contact as he leaned forward and tilted the chalice towards Diego's lips. Diego trembled, causing the wine to spill a little down his chin, however Chris kept his composure and wiped the wine off his chin with his linen cloth. As he did, he whispered, "Hey, wait for me after."

After the service, Diego collected his packs and hovered near the vestry. He didn't have to wait long for Chris – he'd whipped off his ceremonial clothes and was now wearing a hoody, jeans and a large grin across his face.

"So that was your appointment!" said Diego.

"Yep, it was a real honour to have been asked." Chris glanced over his shoulder in the direction of a stairway. "Let me show you something."

"Where are we going?"

"You'll see," stated Chris as he turned and strode across the nave towards the direction of the stairway. A rope barrier blocked the foot of the stairs, but Chris flashed a pass at the security guard and she lifted the rope and kept Diego's luggage for safekeeping. Chris led the way up some steep steps and though Diego felt his legs aching after his morning's hike, he followed after Chris, intrigued. The rooftop was constructed as a granite terrace, and Chris guided Diego across it to take a closer look at the statue of St. James. The saint was mounted facing the main plaza and, in the breeze, Diego sensed the statue's cape flapping.

Chris turned his gaze up to St. James. "Whenever I have any doubts, I come up here and gain strength."

"I get it," replied Diego nodding at the apostle.

"Well, let me show you a view of the plaza, it's really awesome."

Chris made for the clock tower and after climbing a few more steps they went out onto a balcony that wrapped its way around the tower. Diego raised one hand towards his hat and placed the other on the ledge.

"*Sí*, that's awesome!" exclaimed Diego as he leaned over and looked down at the Praza do Obradoiro, brilliantly bathed in the noon sunshine. His eyes followed the stream of pilgrims arriving into the plaza and their eager movements to look upwards at the cathedral. Briefly, his attention was distracted by the flapping sound of wings. Turning and looking up he saw a kestrel hovering close to the tower. Its wings fanned in the updraft and its flight seemed effortless.

"Look," whispered Diego pointing across to the bird.

Chris smiled and gently nodded in response. The kestrel

tilted and drifted towards the centre of the plaza. Diego followed its flight and as it hovered again, he noticed it wasn't casting a shadow onto the flagstones below. Next, the bird swooped playfully, before climbing back up and circling. Banking close to the rooftops the sun glinted across the kestrel's wings and its shadow appeared across the roof tiles. Then it headed for the blue hills beyond. Diego continued to watch it until it got smaller and smaller and disappeared into the blue background.

Diego gazed back down at the square. Cyclists were dismounting, walkers were dropping to their knees and others embraced their companions. With the sun high overhead, they had no shadows either. Chris continued to watch the activity below and after a minute or two Diego said, "Ready to go?"

"Sure, but is there anything you want to leave behind up here… before we go?"

"Leave behind?"

"In medieval times, pilgrims were allowed on the roof to burn things in a stone furnace – signifying the end of their journeys and the deaths of their old selves. Often they burned their clothing. Then, like the *Botafumeiro* ceremony with the incense, it was for practical reasons too. Of course, you can't burn your clothes up here any longer." Chris winked conspiratorially. "But if you want to burn something for old times' sake, I'll grant you that indulgence."

Diego laughed. "Thanks, but I think I'll pass. My wardrobe is pretty bare these days."

They headed towards the tower, down the stairs and collected Diego's things. Leaving the cathedral Chris said, "Do you want to check out the end of the world?"

"You mean Finisterre."

"Yep, I still have a couple of days left before my classes resume. And I was thinking, if you didn't fancy burning your clothes on the rooftop of the cathedral, we could instead take a swim in the ocean."

"Does a bus go there?"

Chris nodded. "I believe so."

"Good, because my legs are finished off by all those stairs. But you're on if we can take the bus."

Chris grinned, "Tomorrow then, we'll freeze our *cojones* off in the Atlantic!"

Diego smiled and Chris led him across the plaza and towards the seminary and its adjoining hostel where he would get a room for the night. As soon as Diego lay down on the clean sheets of the bed, he fell asleep and slept the rest of the afternoon.

THE EDGE OF THE WORLD

Diego and Chris cut across the length of the sandy beach until the town of Finisterre was barely visible behind the dunes. At the shoreline, they placed their shoes and packs on the sand and stepped ankle-deep into the cool water. Their view was a glistening green-blue sea extending into a water-colour blue sky, streaked by thinning clouds. Occasionally other pilgrims arrived at the shoreline, and they watched them as they performed the last rites of their journey. Some removed the scallop seashells that had been tied to their packs and threw them into the breakers and others ran joyously into the sea.

After a while, Chris said, "Are you ready?"

"Guess so!"

Chris pulled off all his clothes and splashed into the sea. Diego hesitated and looked up and down the beach. But it was uninhabited, apart from a couple of pilgrims further along it. He removed all his clothes. Then he yelled, "¡*Madre mía!*" as he tossed his hat onto the sand and jumped through the waves. Diego followed Chris through the higher waves, and as they laughed and cried with childish excitement, Diego soon forgot about the cold.

They floated on their backs and felt as if they were the only two people in the world. They gazed back at the coastline and the steep green hills rising above the beach. Surrendering their aching limbs to the salty water they let themselves be carried by the swell. Sometime later, when the sun was shimmering across the treeline and rippling the clouds a candy pink, Chris tilted his head to one side and asked, "Diego, have you been baptised?

"I believe I was as an infant, when my Mamá was still alive, though I remember I was never confirmed." Diego laughed, "My papá had fallen out with the Church by then."

"I could rebaptise you and perform the confirmation immediately afterwards."

"Well, if you could finally rid me of all my sins, why not!"

Chris grinned and glanced up at the sky. "Well, only God can do that, buddy. But I do know how to perform a water baptism. That would score you some points with him. At the very least it would wash away all the grime from the road."

Diego felt some rocks rub against his feet and he realised the tide had carried them back towards the shore. "Well, I was wondering what kind of ritual I'd perform when my road reached its end. So, why not; it would be an honour to be baptised by Chris the Baptist!"

They swam closer to the shore, and when the sea was at waist height, Chris nodded at Diego. Chris stood beside Diego and placed a hand on the front of his shoulder. Diego rested his strumming hand on his heart and closed his eyes. Gently Chris pushed Diego backwards and submerged him in the water. Diego heard Chris say the familiar words of the baptism prayer, "I baptise you in the name of the Father…" but just as he hit the water, he thought he heard Chris add, "…Your journey has found favour with God." When Diego came up out of the sea, it stilled between waves. He caught his breath, and as the last shards of sun sparkled across the settling ripples, he glimpsed an image. What he saw was the unblemished face of a young woman, ringed by a halo. A wave broke onto the shoreline and they waded back to the beach.

They remained naked as the sun sank into the sea. Two silhouetted figures, looking at the horizon, the broader of the two silently reciting the Confirmation prayer, and the slimmer man understanding that a mother's love is eternal. The wind that followed the sunset helped dry them off before they reached for their clothes.

When they had dressed Diego said, "I guess after those large beach baptisms there's normally music and celebration?"

"Yep, typically," replied Chris.

Diego glanced at his guitar case lying in the sand, then shrugged his shoulders. "But you know what, I'm not feeling in the mood right now. I'm enjoying the silence. He glanced further along the bay to Finisterre's lighthouse. "Plus, I'd like to make the final climb of the Camino."

Chris smiled. "Buddy, you should. Do whatever you feel in the mood for… I'm feeling hungry; I'm going to get something to eat at that café, where we can take the bus. I'll wait for you there."

Diego nodded and they collected their packs. He left Chris in Finisterre and headed out of town along his final road towards the headland and lighthouse. After a couple of kilometres, he passed a stone cross with the Virgin, and he glanced at it and smiled as he began his ascent up the path that led him to the lighthouse. He had no idea what his next move would be or whether he had enough money left in his pocket to buy a bus ticket back to Santiago, but with his guitar by his side, he felt as rich as any man.

Arriving beside the lighthouse, he scrambled down the verge and across the rocks, stopping at the cliff edge. He paused momentarily, then raised a hand to his head, removed his Stetson and curled his fingers around its rim. He shivered, feeling the breeze around his head, but he pulled his arm back anyway. With a flick of his wrist, he launched the hat over the edge of the world. He watched it as it spun like a Frisbee towards moonshine on the water. Then it fell out of sight. His long hair flared over his shoulders, and the sounds of the sea rolled over him, enhanced by the swishes of the wind through the distant Galician forests.

Diego rolled a cigarette and when he had finished smoking, he made his way back up to the lighthouse. With each returning sweep of the beacon, he was brought out of darkness and burned star white.

The heavy rainfall had stopped and the crowd gathered around Bar Paradiso's patio and in the surrounding plaza. They were there to hear the music of the fabled Spanish guitarist. In recent months, news had spread along the Camino roads of the guitarist with wild hair, who wore a dark cloak and wandered the Camino roads.

The rumour, the myth, was that this former flamenco legend had renounced his fortune, and the music he now played had the ability to bring hope and peace to others. It was said that his music was outspoken about the ebb and flow of life; that it was this great river of life doing its job and creating the conditions necessary to acquire wisdom and knowledge along the way. Readying us all for our rebirths.

The guitarist had become known as James the Enlightened, although the people in his village mostly called him Diego, preferring not to translate his name into the English equivalent – including his old friends Ricardo and Javier. They, unlike many of working age, had remained there. More young people had been forced to leave the village as work in the agricultural sector continued to suffer from overseas competition, and jobs became scarce in the region. Subsequently, other businesses in the village suffered, and one of those casualties had been Bar Paradiso. Its final nail in the coffin had been the village *albergue* losing council funding. That meant Arnau lost most of his remaining trade – passing pilgrims – forcing him to close down.

Diego had returned to his village a couple of days after reaching Finisterre to find Bar Paradiso's doors closed and Arnau sitting alone inside looking dejected. The truth was, Diego loved the bar, he loved Arnau and he loved the village. It only took him a moment to grasp that he needed to put the bar back on the map, and the way to do it was to finally have that big concert there. Diego recruited Ricardo and Javier to help organise things, and in turn, they got their wives involved. Their wives had the idea of refurbishing the bar, which was partly funded by Diego selling his Rolex watch and contributing the busking money he received from playing along the nearby Camino paths. The balance was met by generous donations from many of the villagers, who had become excited as soon as they witnessed the refurbishment activity going on at the bar.

This was the bar's grand reopening and the night of the concert, three months after Diego's return. Arnau, with the help of Javier and Ricardo and their wives, was working the bar and serving thirsty customers. Diego came out of the back room with his guitar in hand and paused as he took in the scene. The freshly renovated bar was shining. Arnau wiped his brow with a bar towel and caught Diego's eye. He was working hard and the frown across his face had relaxed, and he nodded blissfully at Diego. Diego winked back at him, stepped over to the doorway and pushed his way through the beaded curtains.

The puddles on the patio reflected the winter stars and Diego stepped around them as he took his place on the patio. He looked out at the crowd. The first person he noticed was Chris, sitting at one of the nearest tables with a beer in his hand. Immediately Diego received a wide grin from him. He figured news of the concert had also reached Santiago. Diego sat down and adjusted the nearby stand so the microphone was close to the guitar.

Just before he closed his eyes, he spotted another pilgrim he knew amongst the crowd. Her wispy hair blew in the cool air as she wended her way through the audience to the front. It was Nessie. Their eyes met and she smiled at him. It was a smile that could only have been reserved for him. It was modest, but in the creases of her face, he saw he was forgiven and he felt her love. He smiled back at her. What was Nessie doing here, now? Had she left her boyfriend? Evidently, word about his concert must have reached her too; had she remained in Spain?

Diego glanced up at San Pedro's bell tower. It was the church his mamá and papá had been married in. The idea of marriage seemed like a possibility again, and he knew the perfect priest to marry him, should that ever happen. He glanced back at Nessie and she gave Diego the rock-on-hand sign. He grinned back at her. Was he about to begin his second life, back here in the village? Had he been afforded a second chance with Nessie? He didn't know. He reckoned when the concert was over and he'd had time to chat to Nessie, he'd be closer to answering those questions. Perhaps he and Nessie could help Arnau with the bar? Arnau was definitely going to need some extra help now. But he reminded himself to breathe and take each day as it comes.

Diego bent his head over his guitar and closed his eyes. Then he took a breath and drew his guitar in close to his chest. He still didn't know if his flamenco hit the heights of *duende*. But that no longer mattered. All that mattered was playing what was in his heart. This song would be for Nessie.

I can still remember that first night and morning in St. Jean Pied de Port, the starting point for the classic Camino route to Santiago de Compostela, Galicia. Then I was a novice pilgrim. The nocturnal noises of some fifty pilgrims I'd been sharing a dormitory with had kept me awake most of the night – I was on a top bunk, and my earplugs were below me in the darkness, deep inside my backpack.

So I was in a daze from a lack of sleep when I joined the throng of pilgrims at dawn. But I can still hear the clackety-clack of the trekking poles against the cobblestones as we left town and followed the Camino path into the foothills of the French Pyrenees. Birds of prey soared high in the thermals and wild horses grazed alongside the trail. It was a mystical experience; it almost felt like a dream. Yet, I have my pilgrim *credencial* to prove that it was real.

I have walked some 1,500 kilometres along the Francés, Finis-terre, Mozárabe, and Portugués Caminos through Spain and Portugal.

The Reluctant Pilgrim series is inspired by those adventures. Whether fictional pilgrims or real people, I've discovered that all pilgrims along the Camino roads share a common spirit – the compulsion to walk. Creating the space to observe life and contemplate their place in it. Ultimately choosing their own paths. I hope these books spark within you the desire to embark on your own Camino journey; you'll know when the time is right.

ENJOYED THIS BOOK?

YOU CAN MAKE A BIG DIFFERENCE

Reviews are the most important way of spreading the word about my books. And readers, like you, are kindly making a big difference by sharing their views.

So if you enjoyed this book, I would be very grateful if you could spare a few moments more by jumping over to the website of the store where you bought the book, and leaving a short honest review too.

By sharing your review, you will be bringing my books to the attention of other readers, which will help me continue to build a loyal readership.

Thank you so much.

ACKNOWLEDGEMENTS

I'd like to thank Emma Carmichael, who joined me again for another Camino, this time the Portugués. I would have missed so much if you hadn't been walking beside me. You also went the extra mile by joining the proofing and formatting team – I couldn't have done it without you babe! There are also my other travel companions – the people I met along the Camino path – too many to mention: from the pilgrims to the hospitality workers, I thank you for your friendship and inspiration.

A big hug to Bill Traugott for his honest feedback and helping me craft my initial draft and turn it into a story. You have a unique talent for deciphering my words and suggesting what I was really trying to say.

Much gratitude to my team of brothers, Calvin Niles, Brian O'Toole and Shack Baker for continuing to believe I had this book inside me.

Thank you Tatiana Wilde for your editing service, and thanks to Leonora Meriel, Adam Wells and Bridget Carmichael for your proofing assistance. And cheers to my loyal Street Team for coming on board at the last minute and picking up errors that had slipped through the editing process.

A huge thanks to my art and design team, firstly Stuart Bache of Books Covered for this latest cover and creating a fantastic brand for the series, and Ed Zhao for producing another map that any pilgrim would find handy.

Gracias Paco de Lucía and Camarón de la Isla for your flamenco beats, which kept me entertained throughout several drafts. May you both rest in peace.

Finally, many thanks to Paco for sharing your home in Granada with me; Rhoswyn our van, for taking me to some outdoor writing locations; the city of Santiago de Compostela; and as, always, my readers for giving me a reason to keep writing – your support and interest is always appreciated.

ABOUT THE AUTHOR

The wanderlust of Stephen R. Marriott, a British author, began in his childhood growing up in Portishead in the West Country of England. He has spent time in London working in stockbroking, but his writing career began with his journey on the Camino de Santiago. This pilgrimage awakened his creativity and formed the basis of his debut novel, *Candyfloss Guitar*, book one of the *Reluctant Pilgrim* series.

His craving to travel remains, and when he needs to break out from his office, he'll often jump into his van, Rhoswyn, and take to the road. So far, she's proven more than a suitable space for writing.

You can connect with Stephen online at:
www.stephenrmarriott.com.

Through email at: stephen@stephenrmarriott.com

Or why not connect with him on social media:

facebook.com/StephenRCommunity
instagram.com/stephenrmarriott

JOIN MY COMMUNITY

If you haven't joined my community yet, I'd like to invite you.

**You can join my Community
by signing up at my website:**

www.stephenrmarriott.com

Building a relationship with my readers is the best thing about writing. I send free monthly newsletters about my discoveries along the way (I travel a lot and live in my van part of the year) including travel tips, book recommendations and off the beaten path experiences. Plus, occasional emails with details of new publications, free books and community events.